FA
Ch
VIR

Aashish Chopra is an award-winning viral video marketer, having made and marketed videos with millions of shares and gazillion views. His videos have hit 350 million views, with one becoming Asia's most-shared branded Facebook post and another hitting 40 million views in a week. He's a sought-after speaker on viral video marketing and was featured in *Forbes*. He heads content marketing at Ixigo.

'Aashish, through this book, brings life to the art of content creation. What was until now considered the haven of only creative mavericks has been democratized by Aashish, inspiring all of us to produce content that touches people's emotions. This is a timeless book, the prescriptions of which will last even when the medium of distribution has changed.' – **Ankur Warikoo, CEO and co-founder of Nearbuy**

'I've been fortunate to have Aashish on our team, offering me a ringside view of his journey of mastering the art of storytelling, perfecting the science of video making, and using the creative power of content to create a bridge of empathy between brands and consumers, resulting in millions of content shares and oodles of customer love for Ixigo. Aashish's frugal and humane approach to building share-worthy content instead of ads offers a disruptive way of building a brand by gaining trust and respect.' – **Aloke Bajpai, CEO and co-founder of Ixigo**

'A natural storyteller, an animated speaker and a truly gifted artist, Aashish is a leader with a noble heart. Aashish's strength lies in how he challenges himself and the team to find the best creative solutions, accepting ideas from wherever they may come from – customers, clients, the team, even thin air. Aashish's work is so refreshing it reminds me of those drinks you enjoy – nose-tickling and effervescent!' – **Shilpa Dureja Puri, General Manager (Digital), Samsung India**

'In a world of clutter and too much information, Aashish makes things simple and specific while still being creative and innovative. What more could you possibly ask for.' – **Papa CJ, award-winning comedian and motivational speaker**

'If the top ad-film directors in 2000's were people like Dibakar Banerjee, Prasoon Joshi, Sunhil Sippy, Budhayan Mukherjee, today you hear of young talented "digital-first" video makers like Aashish Chopra. What is amazing about Aashish is that he is the complete package – from writing scripts, shooting, editing and finally, handling awesome content distribution, he and his team have been prolific is showing Indian Internet companies how to growth hack into video marketing and that too frugally! If you are interested in breaking through the clutter and capturing the elusive attention span of customers, there can be no better book for you to read than *Fast, Cheap and Viral*. I would strongly recommend you read this to win the battle for eyeballs, and discover how Aashish and his team regularly create videos that are watched by millions of viewers.' – **Apurva Chamaria, Chief Revenue Officer, RateGain and bestselling author of** *Master Growth Hacking* **and** *You are the Key*

'Aashish Chopra has continuously demonstrated how creativity and insights win over production value in creating content. The viral videos made in-house, under his leadership, are exemplary – a case study in itself. His passion and ownership shows up in his work. If you care about marketing, your brand should be powered with content, and Aashish is the person you'd want on your side and not as your competition.' – **Deepali Naair, Director – Marketing, India and South Asia, IBM**

'Every page of this book is a gold mine in its own might. I see a beautiful and crisp translation of action to words, which I have come to realize is far more difficult than turning words to action. I can see how years of hard work and experience has been woven into this magnum opus of content marketing. From understanding the attention span of viewers to identifying your business values and finding the right meld between the two – this publication covers everything. I love how Aashish has been unabashed about his writing style, making it a true doppelganger of his personality. Every single instance of his life, and the lessons he got out of it have been metamorphosed into actionable outcomes for everyone curious in our field of play. The chapters are crafted in a very crisp and concise manner as in the author's words – our 'BS horizon' is limited. Brilliant perspective, thought-provoking episodes, an easy read and, yes, the icing is humour. This book will be the next chartbuster! Good luck to Aashish, who has realized early on in life that sharing knowledge is the ultimate path to nirvana, and that nirvana is quite a no BS zone. **– Hitesh Malhotra, Chief Marketing Officer, Nykaa**

'Aashish's work reflects a maturity that very few creative people in the business can boast of. Aashish is a true digital native, a brand champion and a master storyteller. In one word, he was born to be viral. And viral and cheap are but two sides of the same genius. I wish him all the best and am looking forward to seeing more of his work, in the years to come.' **– Rameet Arora, Chief Operating Officer (Digital Business),** *Hindustan Times*

'Aashish Chopra is someone everyone in the marketing and advertising world should look up to (I do) for inspiration and learning. In this digital world, he has demonstrated time and again how relevant, engaging content is a secret weapon every brand can possess, but very few actually do. His campaigns over the years are a masterclass of producing entertaining, on-brand creative without having to resort to budget-busting production values. His work for Ixigo has been a cornerstone for communication strategy.' – **Lakshmipathy Bhat, Vice President – Marketing Communications, Robosoft**

'Aashish is one of the only people in the industry who has not only mastered the art and science of video promotion, but also solved the challenge of production cost. No wonder he is able to repeatedly get hundreds of millions of views for the videos he and his team create, and that too at a fraction of typical production cost.' – **Pradeep Chopra, CEO and co-founder, Digital Vidya**

'I have known Aashish's work before I got to know him. Aashish has a deep understanding of the subject and a huge respect for changing market dynamics. He is always experimenting and figuring out what the latest trend is, and this is probably what gives him an edge above others. The ability to understand his audience and their needs and then solve their issues in the simplest possible way is Aashish's specialization. Another thing that stood out for me was his sense of loyalty for the brand he is associated with. I am glad he finally decided to come out and write a book to share his secrets of creating amazing and viral content.' – **Vinay Singhal, CEO and co-founder of WittyFeed**

FAST
Cheap
&
ViRAL

How to Create Game-Changing
Content on a Shoestring Budget

AASHISH CHOPRA

First published in 2019 by Hachette India
(Registered name: Hachette Book Publishing India Pvt. Ltd)
An Hachette UK company
www.hachetteindia.com

SRD

ISBN 978-93-5195-275-6

Hachette Book Publishing India Pvt. Ltd
4th/5th Floors, Corporate Centre,
Plot No. 94, Sector 44, Gurugram 122003, India

Typeset in Cardo 11.5/15
by InoSoft Systems, Noida

Printed and bound in India by
Manipal Technologies Limited, Manipal

MIX
Paper from
responsible sources
FSC™ C104740

For everyone who's afraid of taking the path
less taken

'Ideas are cheap. Ideas are easy. Ideas are common. Everybody has ideas. Ideas are highly, highly overvalued. Execution is all that matters.'

– Casey Neistat

Contents

Introduction

My Story

It was a crisp February morning in 2014. My boss called me into his cabin and after looking at me seriously for a moment, he said, 'We're letting you go.' The company was downsizing or something; but all that mattered to me at that moment was that I had no job. I remember driving back home that day, in my tiny Tata Nano, swishing past the BMWs on the highway, wondering what had just happened. With tears in my eyes, I tried to focus on the road ahead (almost metaphorically). I realized I had to act fast to realize what the hell I wanted to do. I did not have a degree (I dropped out of college in my second year), and living through the taboo of being degree-less in India meant building my own skills, fighting my fears and insecurities, creating my own little raft and charting out a new path. I had started building websites in Class 9, taught web design right after school, volunteered abroad, started and shut down a business in Canada, and had done my time deep diving into creating thousands of infographics and understanding content marketing. Oh, and I attended a film school too (for three months, and then I spent another six months unlearning half the things I had been taught for they did not apply to the fast-changing world of online video content).

Just like how a disability can lead people to build other strengths, I wanted to make my absence of a degree and my job insecurity so irrelevant that it wouldn't matter any more. Now at that point, for a whole year I had been thinking (more like procrastinating) about making a video. With no options to fall back on, no job, no prospects, nor the blessings of any guru, I decided it was time I made that video.

The first video

I lived in Gurgaon (now Gurugram) and worked in Delhi. Every single day I had to cross the border, past a massive toll plaza. It was the worst thing to have to do every morning, with thousands of slow moving cars clogging the lanes, traffic piling up and frustration running high among the thousands of commuters. The idea that had been brewing in my head for a year was to capture a random act of kindness on video. When my car reached the toll plaza, I gave the guy ₹42 instead of ₹21 (the toll amount), with a Post-it note that said, 'I have paid your toll. Have a great day ☺'. I asked the person manning the toll plaza to give it to the car behind me when it came up, and I drove on. It was a random act of kindness, and I hoped that if one person started, it would create a tiny wave of happiness. In preparation, I had put my ideas down in bullet points, written multiple ways to execute my plan, and come up with many versions of the script. I placed three cameras on my car, drove across the toll plaza many times, each time paying the toll for the cars behind me. I captured it all on video and came home to edit it for a couple of hours until the whole thing came together in a very simple video. It focused on the core of the idea, with no useless storytelling to distract viewers. Then I uploaded it.

Happy accident?

'Your video is on NDTV's homepage!' my wife shouted over the phone. Before I could grasp what she was saying and before I could frantically fire up my browser to check, there was a knock on the door. 'Radio Mirchi is looking for you,' blurted out my colleague, her voice bubbling with excitement. Radio what! The video which I had uploaded to YouTube last evening, and shared on Facebook had hit the stratosphere. I was about to taste the success of creating an actual viral video. Since I was in the video, everywhere I went in the city people started recognizing me – waving from their cars, strangers walking up to me in cafes to shake my hand. Google 'Gurgaon Toll Surprise' and you'll see the first page peppered with links about the video.

This was the happiest and the scariest time of my life. Happiest because of the tiny 15 seconds of fame I had achieved. People were recognizing me on the streets; I didn't change my clothes for three days! Scariest because if I did not build on this, or figure out why the video worked, I'd become a one-hit wonder and would soon evaporate from the public's mind. This break had come after a long wait; a decade of working in the darkness, starting and closing businesses, experimenting with videos; from working in sales to managing social media accounts. Little did I know my career had taken a new direction, and that this was the first day of the rest of my life.

A viral video to me was nothing but a happy accident, when the stars were aligned and luck was shining bright. That day, I started my journey in learning the method to the madness behind viral videos. And, as I kept going, I kept recording what I learnt on the notes app on my phone. Whatever I observed from the first video I applied to the next, which, once again went viral. I did some experiments, and a third went viral. This one exploded in such a way that it blew my mind. A video made in August of 2014 clocked 7 million views; it was shared by 350K (3.5 lakh) people and reached 25 per cent of the Facebook Internet user base in India! The same video became Asia's most-shared branded Facebook post and went on to win awards.

The notes in my phone kept increasing, and I knew, somewhere at the back of my head, that the day these videos stop going viral, would be the day I was done, and I would find myself running the rat race again. So the need to experiment and record all that I learnt became an obsession. In a span of one year, multiple videos went viral and hit millions of views. Some even travelled far beyond physical borders and hit millions of views in China! In five years, the videos I helped produce would cross 350 million views, get me a mention in Forbes, lead me to win many awards and get me slots to give lectures at IITs and IIMs. F**k the degree.

No *gyaan* or brain farts

This book is a culmination of all those 'best practices' I noted down, and have learnt about creating viral videos. The actionable tips from these cases will make for a definitive guide for viral success. There's no theoretical *gyaan* in this book, but actual learning, born out of true experiences. So no BS here. And these strategies not only apply for videos but for content as a whole, because the game is not about technology or platforms, but about user behaviour and changing the way we think about marketing.

Before I began this project I remember walking through bookstores and scanning titles on Amazon looking for books that told the story of content marketing insights coming from India, and I was surprised to find that there was very little available. There is no book from India that tells the story of how businesses and brands can adapt and evolve in the fast-changing world of social and content marketing. For too long we've been aping the West, now it's time for India to rise and knock the socks off the world. It is time we debunk the traditional approach to marketing and learn the rules of the new game.

One more thing...

I wrote this, not just to have a book with my name on it – this wasn't born out of a self-obsessed wish of being an author or to make a shiny addition to my business card. I wanted this to be my manual of sorts, documenting all the fundamentals I learnt from constant experiments – the best practices validated by millions of views over the years. There are many books on social media, content and marketing, and I didn't want this to be another brain fart about theories or tips curated from the Internet. I wanted this to be a practical guide to viral content marketing; a reference I can look back on when I'm 70 and losing my memory, wondering about the impact I had in this life and how many people I managed to empower. This is for the younger me, millions of whom are travelling in trains, working hard and trying to understand how to build their careers and disrupt traditional ideas with kick-ass creativity. This is for every marketing manager who thinks they need to be more creative, or who thinks only creative agencies have that holy power vested in them. This is for every student who wants to stand out and for every chief marketing officer (CMO) who wants to lead marketing teams and not have to depend on agencies to get work done. This is for everyone who wants to build in-house capability and wow those who think they are the gatekeepers of creativity or marketing.

Even before I started writing, I validated every key point listed here not just by the millions of views the videos received, but from professionals across the board. I've spoken at India's top institutions, at India's top marketing conferences and done tons of masterclasses, and tried to ensure I'm able to answer every question from the thousands of people who show up at these events. I've answered questions from students about how Facebook works to questions from top CMOs in the country, people who are respected in the industry, with years of experience, about how to leverage video content, and from start-ups about how to reach millions of viewers on ridiculously low budgets. I'm as thankful for every stupid question as I am for the challenging questions (it's always good to ask stupid questions; it's better to look stupid for two minutes than to be stupid forever!) I have been asked. Those questions helped solidify the foundation of this book, and for that I'm grateful.

If you have read this far, you're ready to dive into the next chapter, and half my battle is won. I promise to answer any questions you may have about things not covered in the book, only if it has been part of my truth or experience. To bulls**t is easy; but to have things that work, you need true experience. You have the right to get in touch with me, tweet or send me a message with your questions, thoughts and suggestions. I'm with you on your journey of growth if you're committed to it yourself; else, I've got a million things to do of my own.

Time to hit the road. Every chapter is like a milestone and there will be many pit stops along the way in the form of tiny insights, quotes and actionable reminders. We will learn everything from understanding the massive opportunity for video and content, to recognizing the challenges that come with those opportunities. How to think viral, and how to pick topics. How to design the content for maximum engagement and still keep it low budget. How to distribute your content, and not just hope it will get picked up and do well on its own. Also, we will learn about applying my fundamentals for personal branding and taking your career into high gear with the power of content marketing.

Fasten your seatbelt, or grab your coffee, it's time to vroom vroom!

PART I

THE BIG
PICTURE

Massive Opportunity for Marketing

On a lazy weekday evening in 1996 – back from school and trying not to deal with the homework pressures of Class 8 – I was tinkering with my dad's personal computer, which he had bought for his work. The doorbell rang and my elder cousin walked in, bringing with him the coolest gadget I had seen, making my geeky little eyes light up. It was a dial-up modem, which, when connected to the computer and phone line, took me into a magical universe. I was hooked, even though it was not the Internet as we know it today – it was slow and sloppy, and worked off a telephone line. The browser wasn't Chrome or Firefox, but text based and only opened Yahoo until I figured out, after many days of hits and misses with keyboard commands, how to browse the rest of the web.

At school, armed with new quips and one-liners, which I had printed out, this nerdy kid suddenly found himself with ammunition to become the coolest guy in class. From cracking jokes in conversations to being able to print tiny diagrams that made physics look simple, my world had been transformed. Friends came over to gawk at my new-found window to the world, and staying over became about browsing the web, chatting anonymously with strangers across the world and sending emails. I was the first in my class to have an email address, a swanky Hotmail account, which I promptly got printed on my 'business card'. The card had my name, address, email and a cool little logo, and I felt ready for the world.

The Internet party at home, however, had just one problem – my mother. She would suspiciously look at me working on the computer late into the night. 'What are you doing?' she'd ask, and I'd reply with what I had heard dad say: 'Working'. She would come into the room every hour to ask when I would turn the Internet off, invading my privacy – a relatively new concept for me – while surfing online. Since the Internet worked off a phone line, our monthly phone bill reached shockingly high amounts, further worrying my mom.

What gave me away was a tiny light on the cordless phone receiver in my parents' room, which kept blinking when the phone was in use, indicating I was online. Desperate to reclaim my space, I was washing my face just before hitting the bed one night, tense from all the policing of my freedom, when there in the mirror I saw my solution. My eyes lit up like a plotting villain in a movie – mom's bindi. The tiny circular thing could be stuck anywhere, even on that blinking light on the phone receiver.

After laughing evilly to myself (in a whisper), I quietly tiptoed into their room and placed the black bindi on the blinking light, camouflaging it with the phone receiver. Now my nights were police-free, the Internet was on full throttle and the phone bill...well, who cared about the phone bill! That was the beginning of what was about to become a revolution.

The Internet took the world by storm. Dial-up Internet gave way to DSL (Digital Subscriber Line) and text browsers became the swanky web browsers of today. The dot-com era saw the rise of Silicon Valley in the US, with new websites and ideas gaining momentum. In India, the Internet was still a fancy thing at the time; the barrier to entry for the masses being the ability to own a computer and the know-how of using it. Using the Internet as an option for marketing was new and e-commerce was still a far-fetched dream. As Internet users grew in the US and the rest of the western world, India was happy with Indian-origin entrepreneurs killing it in Silicon Valley. Heck, Sabeer Bhatia was my superhero! (Remember the guy who sold Hotmail for $400 million to Bill Gates?)

The rising giant

Fast forward a few years, and the fancy little Internet of the past has become the biggest force in business today, powerful enough to topple regimes. What was a luxury has become a necessity. The total Internet user base in India is estimated to cross 700 million by 2020[*]; that's almost two in every three Indians with access. And by 2030, India will have more than a billion Internet users! Google India's Managing Director shared at their annual event in 2018 that every month about 10 million new Internet users get on the bandwagon.[†] India's Internet user base is skyrocketing and will soon

---

[*] NASSCOM, 'The Future of Internet in India', August 2016.

[†] 'India is adding 10 million active Internet users per month: Google', *Business Standard*, 27 June 2018.

beat China's. Further, more than 80 per cent users access the web on their mobile devices.* No fancy computers to purchase, no commands to learn, and none of that keyboard and mouse business. Mobile phones with their touch interface have changed the way we imagine the Internet. An entire generation of users completely skipped the desktop Internet era and is experiencing the Internet for the first time on their mobile devices.

My mom doesn't know how to use a mouse and keyboard to save her life, but on her mobile, I worry she'll crash Facebook and WhatsApp with her 'Good morning' messages! Millions of Indians are jumping on the Internet bandwagon, armed with low-cost smartphones and cheap data. And the amount of time users are spending on the Internet is taking them away from traditional media such as the radio, newspapers and the once-almighty television. Those were the days of one-way traffic, where content was streamed into our homes and

'By 2030, India will have more than a billion Internet users.'

---

* Ananya Bhattacharya, 'Internet use in India proves desktops are only for Westerners', *Quartz India*, 30 March 2017.

7

we were passive consumers. Now, the streaming of content happens on tiny interactive devices and we are able to participate, like, comment, share and engage with it. Things are far more democratic, but also far scarier for big brands who are used to one-way communication.

The mobile-first generation

I remember when I came back from Canada (after starting and shutting down a business), I took a trip on the overly crowded Delhi metro. It was a very different India in which I found myself, compared to the one I had left. Almost every person had a smartphone – some fancy, others low-cost. People who made ₹10,000 a month had a smartphone and people who made ₹2,00,000 had one too. It was the great equalizer.

'India has the second largest number of smartphone users in the world.'

Your driver uses WhatsApp same as you, your milkman may have more friends on Facebook than you. My mom has a group on WhatsApp of her old school friends, where they play 'Antakshari' – one person posts an audio clip of a song and the others respond with another clip. My friend who owns a business runs it entirely on WhatsApp. My boss sends updates to me on WhatsApp, and so does my dhobi when my clothes are ready. I check Twitter the instant there's an earthquake, Uber and Ola cabs are a tap away, and I've had the experience of drivers asking me how to setup websites to start other businesses. Movie bookings happen on mobile apps, as does selecting a restaurant for dinner. From flights to trains, everything can be booked through the tiny little computers in our pockets.

A report from Mary Meeker (a venture capitalist; her much-awaited annual Internet Trends report gives an overview of the entire industry) in 2017 stated that Indians spend 28 hours on their mobile phones, four hours on TV and two hours on print every week.* Internet speeds have reached 4G from 2G, and it has almost become a basic right to have connectivity today; so much so that in Delhi, 'free Wi-Fi' was a political promise made to win elections! If you check the top five most downloaded apps in the country, all five are social networking apps. Imagine millions of people, who have super cheap smartphones, which can

---

* Kleiner Perkins Caufield & Byers and Mary Meeker, 'Internet Trends 2017', 31 May 2017.

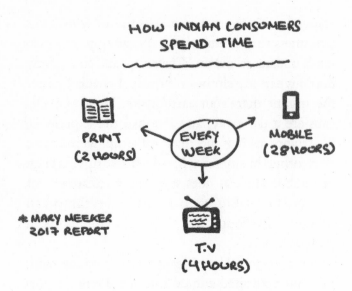

HOW INDIAN CONSUMERS
SPEND TIME

PRINT
(2 HOURS)

EVERY
WEEK

MOBILE
(28 HOURS)

* MARY MEEKER
2017 REPORT

T.V
(4 HOURS)

run at least four apps, have social networking apps as their most frequented two apps. India has already beaten the US to become the number one country in terms of number of Facebook users. Our WhatsApp user base is already in the multi-millions, LinkedIn has become the Facebook of the business world and just check Twitter any moment to see how it is shaping public opinion. Powering this phenomenal growth is the rapid adoption of smartphones, with India having the second largest number of smartphone users in the world (and it's only a matter of time before we become the largest).

Social media consumption on mobile devices is increasing rapidly across the country. Everyone is hooked to their phones, day and night, sharing videos, memes, articles, photos and breaking news. The mobile revolution is completely changing the way we reach out to our users.

The power of content

At the centre of this massive storm is the rapid consumption of content. From updates on Facebook to funny jokes and memes on WhatsApp, everywhere you look people are consuming and sharing content at a rapid pace. Social media provides an open and democratic platform, but content is at the centre of it all. Content is what you're consuming when checking reviews of a product on Amazon, it is the content of a video that compels you to share it with your friends, it is content in an open letter that incites you to take action, it is content again that you forward to your school alumni groups on WhatsApp, and content that attracts users to share and like your article on LinkedIn. Social media has made content so powerful, that you hold the power to influence millions in the palms of your hands. With every smartphone capable of creating audio–visual content and distributing it far and wide through an app, all you need today is a story, and you have your own way of going 'viral'.

Content marketing on steroids

With the whole concept of media being disrupted in the last decade, and social networking apps taking up most of the time in a user's life, content marketing has become the new playing field for marketers. Wherever user attention goes, the marketing budget follows. And viral marketing is like content marketing on steroids. It's about catapulting your

'Viral marketing is like content marketing on steroids, and videos are dominating newsfeeds everywhere.'

content to reach and engage with millions. Posting something on social media is one thing, but when your users start spreading your content like wildfire, when shares and comments on your content start snowballing, that's viral marketing. Any piece of content which attracts tons of engagement from social media users, gets its wings to go viral. It could be funny pictures, memes, articles or videos.

In this book, I'm focusing on content marketing with videos, since that's what is dominating user attention everywhere and every social media platform has pivoted to videos in a big way. And when a video goes viral, it helps you save millions by reaching your audience without having to spend on making your content visible. What used to cost crores in TV budgets, can now be achieved in ridiculously low amounts purely through the power of the content. When users actively and rapidly engage with your content, it gains momentum, snowballing into millions of views – something traditional marketers take time to grasp. In my time working at Ixigo, two videos beat TV advertisements in terms of sheer reach, although they were made on incredibly low budgets. Videos have been the emerging trend in marketing year after year. In early 2019, I was invited to speak at the *Hindustan Times* Brand Leadership forum, where almost every CMO present talked about videos and how it was the number one priority for them, something which was missing years before. What started as a trend has become the biggest force in marketing today.

'Achhe din' for Internet marketing

No wonder India is attracting tons of start-up capital and is fast becoming the most exciting place to be in. If you're a student worried about your career or a start-up entrepreneur looking for a growth hack, or if you work or lead marketing for any big or small brand, it is time you accept the reality that the game will be won on mobile phones and social media, and not on TV or print. With all this excitement about 'achhe din' for India, there's a big challenge that comes with it. Something I'm very mindful of every day, something we need to be aware of, when creating content. Let's dive into that.

MASSIVE
OPPORTUNITY
FOR MARKETING

DISRUPTION OF
TRADITIONAL MEDIA

LOW COST
PHONES AND
CHEAP DATA

VIDEOS DOMINATING
NEWSFEEDS

INTERNET
USER BASE
RISING

TIME SPENT
ON MOBILE PHONES
SKYROCKETING

Challenge: Competing with Goldfish

In India, this is the best time to be in content marketing. The tide is in your favour. But with this exciting opportunity there are big challenges to overcome too. We need to always be aware of these challenges when we're creating content, planning campaigns or user-engagement exercises. Once we're super aware of these challenges and focus all our actions towards doing the right things, that's when the magic happens.

Content, content everywhere

Did you know that Facebook can potentially show you 2,000 posts every day? If it starts showing so many posts daily, what will you do? You'll stop using Facebook; there's too much to handle in life already. That's bad for business for the social media platform and so they curate (with the help of a newsfeed algorithm) and show you only what's relevant to you. Take the case of WhatsApp, where there is no filtering. How many WhatsApp groups do you have on mute for an entire year? I have muted every single group, from family groups to old school friends to alumni groups. If they gave us the option for muting the groups for a lifetime, I'd be the first to mute them all. This content chaos is what we sift through daily. In some cases, platforms filter for us and show us what's relevant (Facebook, Twitter, Instagram and LinkedIn, for example), in others we do it ourselves (the WhatsApp mute, for instance). Today, on social media newsfeeds, there is an overwhelming amount of content chaos.

'Today, on social media newsfeeds, there is an overwhelming amount of content chaos.'

I frequently take trips in the Delhi Metro and short-distance trains on my validation exercises, and have noticed that when people have long stretches of time ahead of them, where they are doing nothing, then out come the phones and everyone is busy consuming content. The sea of commuters is hooked to their shiny glass slabs – some playing games, others almost always watching videos. It made me realize that all the effort put into creating content or videos, be it a $2 million project with a celebrity production crew or a low-budget video shot on a phone, is gone with one swipe up of the thumb. Every brand or content creator is competing to stop that thumb from swiping.

'All the effort put into creating videos, be it a $2 million project with a celebrity production crew or a low-budget video shot on a phone, is gone with one swipe up of the thumb.'

The sheer volume of content available adds to the chaos in which the user lives. Further, user behaviour in Tier I cities seems different from that of Tier II cities. For example, Hindi and regional-language content tops the charts in Tier II and Tier III towns, compared to big cities.

Our focus must be to keep in mind that our content will live in chaos, and must be designed to stand out, hold the users' hand and take them on a journey.

There's too much competition

Another big challenge facing content creators and marketers is that there's too much competition in the newsfeed as well. Everyone and their cousin can create content today. Heck, everyone has got a smartphone in their pocket and can shoot HD videos. When the number of content creators increases on a platform, the organic reach keeps decreasing. Since everyone is competing for user attention, platforms start monetizing the reach, their core business pillar – 'distribution'. Platforms incentivize content creators by giving them a lot of visibility in the beginning, which brings them their audience (the user base). Once there are enough content creators, and user behaviour becomes all about spending more time consuming the content, platforms start monetizing the reach. Facebook did it earlier, and now LinkedIn is doing it – giving a lot of visibility if you post videos right now, and, once it becomes mainstream, it's moolah for them, and a chance to milk the 'content distribution' cow.

Many complained when Facebook made updates to their newsfeed algorithm, wherein they gave preference for posts by friends or family members over posts by brands on the newsfeed. The potential for reaching more users decreased for marketers. But, the reality is that it's not just the algorithm changes that affected the reach; the competition has also increased. Suddenly, your branded content is competing with your uncle's unemployed son, who thinks he too can make it big with videos. More power to him, but for marketers this is the new reality – democratic competition with everyone.

The goal then is not just to stand out from the competition, but to create content so compelling that the audience sits up, takes action and engages with it. The bottom line for marketers is to create content and campaigns that stand out from a sea of mediocrity; it must be truly remarkable and thumb-swipe stopping. That's a tall order, but a goal worth striving for. The fittest will survive in this content-eat-content world, and we need to be nothing less than the best to survive. My dad once told me, 'Not failure, but aiming low is a crime'. Only when you shoot for the stars will you reach the

'Only when you shoot for the stars will you reach the moon. If you only shoot for the electricity pole, you'll, at max, be standing on your desk.'

moon. If you only shoot for the electricity pole, you'll, at max, be standing on your desk.

Bulls**t radars have evolved

Remember the India of the early 1990s, when there was one TV in the family and only one TV channel we could all watch? Good old Doordarshan. Watching TV was a social event, and we would all sit around and wait for our favourite programmes to come on. The concept of a remote control did not exist, and when ads came in between programmes...well, we watched them, for what other option did we have? That's why we remember ads from that time, from 'Nirma, washing powder Nirma' to '*Hamara* Bajaj' – we watched them without any option of escape.

Then came cable television, and along with it came the all-powerful remote control. Whenever an ad came on, we were given the power to change the channel. Instead of having to patiently wait for an ad to finish, through the remote control we started our evolution in filtering advertisements and this helped develop our behaviour in avoiding them. It was the beginning of our evolution in detecting BS in the media.

Fast forward, and have you seen how millennials watch videos these days? Their BS radars are so finely evolved that whenever there's an ad, they have 20 different tabs open on their browsers and they start watching something else instantly. Ads by nature are self-promotional, and today's generation can spot such BS content miles away. The remote controls of TVs have evolved to the tabs on our browsers or the apps that we can switch to. Ad-blockers are on the rise in the country, and their numbers keep going up every year, posing a big challenge to all those busy creating ads.

As an audience we have become more perceptive. Take your morning newspaper for example; there's an ad blindness as you check the news. Even if they add 10 pages of ads before the front page, you are likely to start after flipping through them. In my experience, nobody likes to be sold anything: they want to buy when they are ready. Informed or uninformed, users today want a sense of control over what they consume and do not like feeling like they have been manipulated.

We need to be aware of the BS radar of consumers, and instead of looking at the users, must look in the same direction as them. Real and authentic content is what the Internet is built on, and we need the DNA of BS-free authenticity in our content.

Competing with goldfish

Can you guess what the human attention span is today? Eight seconds! Fricking eight seconds! Even goldfish have a nine-second attention span. What that means is that every eight seconds something happens in our environment, which takes our attention away from the task at hand. How many apps do you have on your phone? On an average, a smartphone user has 20 apps on their phone and all of them keep buzzing all day long. Each app is trying to grab your attention.

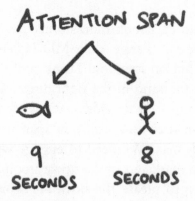

I remember a start-up sent out an iOS emergency notification announcing their latest sale! That's how desperately companies are trying to grab your attention. Just look at the hoardings on busy roads when you're driving. Your car zips past the billboard in a quarter of a second, and it attempts to engage you in that time. In your opinion, what kind of billboard will work better? A board with small font, detailing the 'features' of the product or a board with just one engaging line? The reality is that we live in a super busy, chaotic world. We're reacting to life every minute – from paying bills, thinking about our career, working with difficult bosses, pleasing people, planning our kid's future, planning vacations, taking care of loved ones and taking care of our own health. On top of all of this, our phone keeps buzzing all day long.

I went to Facebook India's office last year and their biggest challenge, their MD explained, was to harness human attention! Thank god! Validation that I was thinking in the right direction. When my team and I create videos, we work with the assumption that user attention span is three to six seconds max. We need to engage with them fast. When marketers in their boardrooms, always attempting to please the boss, are working on campaigns and content, they believe the users are sitting in a movie hall, in the dark, with a two-hour attention span, waiting to appreciate your logo. We need to be aware that attention span is incredibly short and our content must be designed to come to the point real fast.

Platforms control the reach

All social media platforms are in the business of reach. They build a free-to-use product and when they scale up, you realize that all this while *you* were their product. Be it Facebook, or any new shiny app that lets people sing along. When users start spending more time on their platforms, the apps start monetizing this cash cow and begin charging brands for reaching the users. Newspapers, for example, hated it when Facebook asked them to pay to reach their users. These newspapers had worked for decades and decades to build a name for themselves, and Facebook was now charging them to reach out to those very users. Following this, many newspapers started email lists so they could reclaim control over the reach and avoid having to pay unnecessary costs.

To understand how these social media platforms control the reach, imagine this: You are holding a concert and there are millions of people who have come to listen to you. You have the mic in your hands and a million fans in front of you. Now Facebook (or any other social media platform) is the one who controls the volume of the speakers. If you don't pay them, then just the audience in the first row will hear you – that's your organic reach. If you want to reach more rows in the crowd, better cough up the moolah to turn up the volume of the speakers, which is your paid/sponsored/boosted reach. But the kicker is that if what you're performing is awesome, the people in the first row will tell the rows behind and so on, allowing your content to spread like wildfire. And that's how you beat these platforms at their own game, because they are built on the premise of people sharing content and they can't stop that democratic sharing.

So you have two options. Either spend millions to reach your user base (most big-budget brands do that, with lousy ads shoved in our faces all the time, on every platform, until their budgets run out) or make your content so incredibly powerful that it spreads like wildfire, is shared like crazy and becomes 'viral' regardless of a low budget. This is the reason why so many start-ups are killing big brands on social media. As a start-up, when you have little to no budget and are without resources, you're forced to improvise. Creativity shines in times of scarcity. Today, start-ups have the balls to compete with brands with deep pockets because they don't just get customers but evangelists – people who share their content and talk about them. Big brands aren't scared of other big brands today, but rather of teams of eight in a basement somewhere, who can knock their socks off.

REACH vs. VIEWS vs. ENGAGEMENT

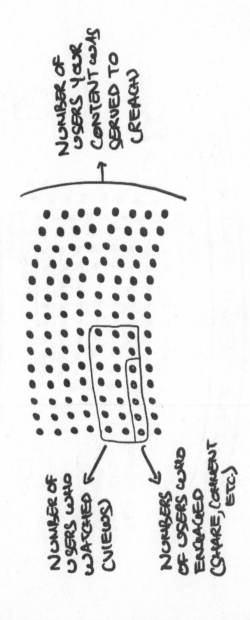

NUMBER OF USERS YOUR CONTENT WAS SERVED TO (REACH)

NUMBER OF USERS WHO WATCHED (VIEWS)

NUMBERS OF USERS WHO ENGAGED (SHARE, COMMENT ETC.)

HOW PLATFORMS CONTROL REACH

YOUR AUDIENCE

SPEAKERS

ORGANIC REACH

YOU

PLATFORMS CONTROL VOLUME OF SPEAKERS

Viral: The wrong focus

'Viral' is the most abused word in the industry today. It has almost become a category of videos/content. Bosses ask for three product videos, one informational and two viral videos – as if virality is in anyone's control. So many people at events ask me about the formula for a viral video, and I, almost every time, tell them, '*Yeh lo* combiflam, *subah tak* viral *ho jayega.*' But when I tell them the process, the method I obsess about, they think there's something I'm not telling them. Everyone wants a shortcut. The truth is that neither I nor anyone else can make a video viral. It is the audience that makes it go viral by sharing it, talking about it and making sure it reaches all corners of the Internet.

We're obsessed with outcomes in this country. Every student has to top their exams, every medal must be a gold medal and every movie must be a blockbuster. Virality

'Results are never in your hands, but your action and performance is.'

is an outcome of a process, and just like how you can't control other results (be it topping exams, or winning a gold medal), this too ain't in your hands. I learnt from my dad that results are never in your hands, but your actions and performance are. All you can do is focus on your performance. If you want to top your exams, you focus on finishing the syllabus in time and then revising what you studied; if you want to get that gold medal, you improve your lap time every week; and if you want a blockbuster, you work on the damn story first! It's like even if I really, really wanted to, I cannot tell you a funny joke. Because *you* decide if it's funny or not; the best I can do is work on the joke structure, the setup and the punchline. The laughter is not in my hands.

Since 'viral' was not in my hands, my obsession turned to focusing on the things I could control. Because hope is not a strategy. I wanted to ensure we got the result we sought. Sometimes, you can get lucky, but every other time, there is a method, a process and a lot of hard work that goes into making videos that go viral.

The next part of the book is about that magical mantra, which when you focus on and obsess about, results in viral success.

CHALLENGE
TOO MUCH COMPETITION
CONTENT CHAOS
WRONG FOCUS: VIRAL
LOW ATTENTION SPAN
BS RADARS EVOLVED

PART II

METHOD TO THE MADNESS

Secret #1

Make it Share-Worthy

The shift from traditional media to social media has opened up the playing field. From Facebook to YouTube, all tools are free to use and anyone with an idea can break the Internet today. The phenomenon of viral videos has become mainstream; so much so, that when you Google the meaning of 'viral', the marketing definition is up there with the medical one. Being low cost, yet with an impact equivalent to that of TV ads, viral videos have become the latest obsession, the Holy Grail, of content marketing.

'Share-worthy', not 'viral'

Viral is a much abused word in the industry today. Look around, every client and every boss today wants a viral video. What they don't understand is that virality is an outcome, and therefore, by nature, not in our hands. Creators don't make a video go viral – incremental user sharing does.

The question I asked myself five years ago (just after my first video went viral) was: 'If a viral video is the outcome I seek, then what should I focus on?'

'Creators don't make a video go viral – incremental user sharing does.'

My boss asked me to make an emotional video once. The objective was to create a patriotic, touching video, slated for release on Republic Day, and I asked myself the same question then: 'If an emotional video is the outcome I want, then what should I focus on?' The right focus for a viral video is to create something that is share-worthy. And boy, the video hit 15 million views, more than 100K people shared it and the Railway Minister of India wrote a poem about it! Google 'Ixigo *Ghar Wali Baat*'; it's a video about train travel in India.

Share-worthiness is the new way to look at content; it's the direction in which to point your metaphorical artillery to win the war. If it isn't share-worthy, you're wasting your time dreaming about viral content. And I'm not preaching from some brain fart I had last night. I speak from experience, my learnings and the truth, validated over countless experiments, which resulted in more than 350 million views of the videos my team and I have created. So if you love the idea of your videos or content going viral, focus your entire strategy towards thinking of ways to make it share-worthy first.

Why is share-worthiness important?

Quite simply, share-worthy content saves you millions in distribution costs by ensuring that content organically reaches your users or audience. Otherwise, the alternative is that the platforms will take your money and distribute it across to their users, and since the content is not share-worthy, there won't be any engagement with it. Though, with time, it may grab many eyeballs, with zero engagement, it will do little for your brand. Your budgets will run out and there will ultimately just be a fancy report where you won't be able to explain to your boss or investor why content marketing has had such little impact on the brand. Spending money is easy, but content engagement is what we need. Even if you spend money to 'boost' or 'sponsor' your content, only when it's share-worthy does organic reach start growing and get you results. Case in point, a video we released a few months ago. To experiment with paid reach, I boosted the video using the entire budget at once. After three days, the video numbers showed how organic reach had hit 75 per cent, since it had garnered 11,000 shares and thousands of comments. Google 'Ixigo Goa Plans be Like' to see the video on Facebook.

When we create content, we want the audience to actively participate, engage and distribute it on our behalf. Since all social media platforms are built on the fundamental of sharing content, they cannot stop people from sharing your videos or content, thus giving you the best bang for your buck – incremental reach and distribution.

'Share-worthy content saves you millions in distribution costs by ensuring that content organically reaches your users or audience.'

The goal of all marketing communication

Our aim is not simply to get the user to stop while scrolling down their newsfeed, but to engage them beyond three seconds. On top of that, we need to get them to watch the entire video, share it, tag their friends and then give us their kidney! While secretly observing people from over their shoulder on one of my many journeys on the metro, it hit me that even though we have all these formats and types of content – long-form content, short-form content, performance ads, bumper ads, six seconders, TV commercials (TVCs), and so on – all that a user sees is 'BS' or 'not BS'. Is it impactful, useful, relatable to my needs or not. It's almost a binary. We need our communication to be BS-free and worthy of sharing, which, I realized, is a tall order.

The goal of all marketing communication today must be share-worthiness. And it's not just for videos. The concept of share-worthiness

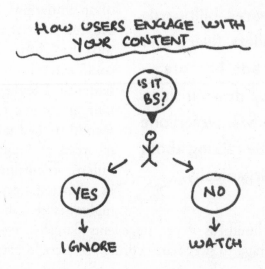

HOW USERS ENGAGE WITH YOUR CONTENT

IS IT BS?

YES → IGNORE

NO → WATCH

applies to your apps, products, services, billboards, mailers, flyers, even TV ads, because deep down inside, you want everyone to be talking about it organically. That's when you know your strategy has worked. Our content should be so awesome that users are meaningfully compelled to share it with their friends.

Over coffee, I once asked a new filmmaker who had joined our team recently, 'What's the most important thing to focus on while creating video content?' Since he had gone over my customary workshop on viral content – sort of an initiation – he blurted out 'share-worthy' before I could even finish my sentence. I looked at him and paused for a second. It had taken me years of countless videos, experiments in validation, sleepless nights before launches and hundreds of speaking events to finally have the courage to say 'share-worthy', so I could back it

'The concept of share-worthiness applies to your apps, products, services, billboards, mailers, flyers, even TV ads, because deep down inside, you want everyone to be talking about it organically.'

up in every question, every strategy meeting with bosses, stakeholders and hecklers in the crowds with insights from my experience. And here was this guy, fresh out of his initiation, ready to conquer the world with the new-found fundamentals of his new boss. More power to him!

Why would anyone care to share?

The one question I ask in all my brainstorming meetings, whether with start-ups, big brands or with my dad (who wants to start making videos for LinkedIn) is: 'Why would anyone share your video?' It's not a difficult question to answer, but it changes our perception and we start looking at everything from the users' perspective, and not from our brand lens, or how cool we think we are.

For me, brainstorming sessions have become a ruthless pursuit of steering ideas in the right direction. Looking back, I have rejected 90 per cent of the ideas from sessions at work or while working with companies since they were not share-worthy. Because focusing on something that is worthy of being shared is about focusing on the interests of users, not on the brand. I've had fights internally about putting users first, branding next. The traditional thoughts regarding branding are rooted in so much self-obsession that we forget that it's the users we're doing this for.

The head of marketing of an e-commerce brand recently asked me at an event, 'People don't trust us. How do we make them trust us?' Well, why would anyone trust you, I asked. Invest in their happiness and well-being, do something for them, before there's an expectation of users doing anything for you. The content you create must make users' lives better and then, my friend, you have a chance at gaining their trust.

Take, for example, LinkedIn recommendations. If you're on LinkedIn, you know how powerful a recommendation can be on your profile. So you ask for recommendations, but don't get too many. Ever wondered why? Ask yourself why anyone would take time out of their schedules to do something for you. Here's a trick: before you ask for a recommendation, write a kick-ass, honest and authentic recommendation for that person. Write the best recommendation he or she deserves, and do some research if you have to. Set the standard and give your best shot at writing that recommendation. Now, you have a chance of a kick-ass recommendation coming back to you, which will make your profile shine for future jobs or business relationships.

Think like a media company

Every company today is first a media company and only then a tech company (or whatever business they are in). They already have fans and followers on their social media profiles; all they need is to keep users meaningfully engaged and grow that follower base. Companies need all their users and audience to be by their side, and so need to give users a reason to share and comment on videos posted. This frees the company from depending on external agencies to drive sales or bring in new users, as their own social media followers are true fans. Eventually it becomes like feeding a dinasour, because as social media followers increase, so would the need to churn out regular content and drive engagement relevant to the brand. Days of simple recall-driven marketing communication are over, we need all our communication to be share-worthy, so our own users and customers become our brand ambassadors and take our message, our brand and our products forward.

Get over yourself

As brands or marketers, we get obsessed with 'us' – our shiny products, our awesome services. The reality is that no one gives a damn about us.

You need to realize that your products or services are not about the company, but rather, about the consumers. I remember seeing posts by a big bank recently asking users what they loved best about their services: a) credit cards b) debit cards c) loans d) offers. Are you kidding me? You think users are waiting at 3 p.m. in the afternoon, wondering why the bank's Facebook posts haven't shown up on their newsfeeds yet? Self-obsessed content (read ads) worked in the times of TV, radio and print media, because it was a one-way form of communication. They broadcasted the ad, and we consumed it.

'You cannot even expect your own team members, co-workers or employees to share your content on social media. You must earn that share.'

Today, we do not just consume, but participate with content. Communication is two-way and nothing short of being the best will work. Today, you cannot even expect your own team members, co-workers or employees to share your content on social media. You must earn that share.

It's not about the views

Numbers: everyone obsesses about the number of views a video has got. Fact is that views can be bought, but engagement is earned. You need to build loyalty and create a user base that is waiting for your next video to come out. No one will share your content because you ask them to. If your boss sends you a mail to share the latest video, you will entertain his/her request two times max before you start to cringe. Social media is a personal space and getting shares by arm-twisting others isn't cool.

What we need is to first get our own people – employees, loyal users, friends – on our side with authentic, kick-ass content, which they will be proud to share.

The next time you see a video which has millions of views, look closely at its numbers. How many shares or comments does it have? If it's all views and no engagement, you can imagine how they burned lakhs of rupees to hit those millions of views, without having anything to show for it, unfortunately. This is typical with brands putting

'Views can be bought, but engagement is earned.'

TV ads on social media – 5 million views, but only 3 shares. Remember, views can be bought, but loyalty is earned. I remember asking a company's brand head about their latest video.

'You have 2 million views on your video, congratulations,' I said.

'Thank you,' he beamed with pride.

'But it has just four shares, how many people do you have in your company?' I asked.

'Two hundred.'

I say, if you can't gain the loyalty of 196 people in your own company, don't expect the world to come love you. And then definitely do not complain that nobody is engaging with your video.

Shares: The new currency for content success

I remember the first time the idea of making 'share-worthy' videos dawned on me. In 2014, a travel hack video we had created was spreading like crazy by the day and, after a few weeks, it went on to become Asia's most-shared branded Facebook post (Campaign Asia report). That one video had 350K shares and almost every person who had shared it had tagged their friends as well. The 350K shares used to creep into my dreams, as I kept wondering if we could ever beat that number. Then, our next video, a simple video about unusual beaches, hit

1.5 million shares. With that strong validation, and results from tons of other experiments, measuring 'shares' became the only metric for content success for me.

Comments are great too, but shares really amplify your message and act like a users' personal endorsement of your content and brand. More than anything, shares are earned, unlike views which can be bought.

'When shares start snowballing, that's when the magic happens.'

So WTF is share-worthy content then?

A writer at *Forbes*, asked me this question recently. The article he was compiling had content marketers from around the world sharing their best practices, and for me it was a 'Bharat *Mata ki jai*' moment, to be able to share my secrets with the world. What makes a video share-worthy, what are ways to pick share-worthy topics? I have five different buckets, or categories of content, which have been validated by millions of views and forms a process, a filter through which all ideas go through before we can get into execution. Time to flip the page and find out what these are.

Secret #2

How to Pick Share-Worthy Topics

For me, picking the right topic is driven by a process and not some random creative 'aha!' moment alone. We need a method to crack that creativity code that leads to viral videos, and not just hope to get lucky every time. It's like deciding the direction in which to lay a railway track. Once you pick the direction and the track is laid, there's no turning back. I've seen many brands take mediocre ideas all the way to the end of the track, without getting anywhere, and burning millions of rupees along the way. I've always been obsessed with finding that equation, that process – a method if you will – to replicate successes in videos, so we are not just shooting in the dark. I'm not saying every idea which comes out of this process will be a super hit, but my method is that we operate like a movie studio – we focus on doing 10 experiments hoping two will work. It's not just creativity, but consistency at being creative that makes the difference. Remember when A.R. Rahman won the Oscar for his song '*Jai Ho*'? Having grown up listening to Rahman, it was my opinion that '*Jai Ho*' wasn't his best song. But one thing I've always loved about Rahman is that he's creative consistently, and that's the quality we need to replicate. You don't know which of your ideas will go on to capture the fancy of the entire world, so every topic we choose must be remarkable, period.

> **'Operate like a movie studio, doing 10 experiments, in hopes that two will work.'**

Defining brand DNA first

Before we dive into brainstorming topics for a video, we need to be very clear about the brand DNA, because that will flow across all the topics we choose for videos or content. It's easy to put a celebrity's face on social media content and get likes, but for meaningful engagement we need the content to be guided by the brand DNA. Brand

DNA lies at the core of every video, every piece of content you publish. It's not just about the category you're in – like travel for Ixigo, food for Zomato or personal finance for HDFC – it's about the larger purpose for a brand to exist. It's about finding the 'why' behind what you do, instead of just 'what' you do. I loved how Simon Sinek in his book *Start with Why* argued that people are inspired by a sense of purpose and the 'why' should come first when communicating, before the 'how' and 'what'. Apple is not about computers, but thinking differently; Nike is not about shoes, but celebrating athletics; Lifebuoy is not about soap, but cleanliness. Finding your brand DNA is about finding out why the brand exists; it is about finding what makes it more than just what its products are. It focuses on how the company plans to change the world. Just like the DNA of a person makes them unique, every brand needs to have a distinct identity.

Now, your product or service can solve one pain point for the user (pain points are things which cause frustration), but in that orbit there are countless other pain points you don't solve, but which your brand can stand for as well. Your brand DNA must not just be about your solution for one pain point, but about making the lives of your users better. And there's a treasure trove of

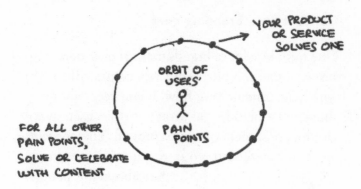

ideas for content, which aligns with your brand DNA. For example, Ixigo solves one pain point of travellers by booking the cheapest flights after comparing fares. All the other pain points of travel, for which we don't provide for, are likely to be associated with our brand DNA, and we solve or celebrate these through our content. You could be in the business of manufacturing and selling light bulbs, but your brand DNA could be about bringing light to the lives of people. Your products solve one pain point, but you have tons of options to create content, driven by the idea of bringing light to the lives of people. Once you have clarity about your brand DNA, then all the ideas you brainstorm will have a unique identity, which helps establish your brand in the long run.

Content first, branding next

One mistake a lot of brands make is masquerading ads as content. Your brand is a conduit through which the content must flow. If you keep obsessing about your brand, you won't see the users who are the consumers of your content. The content must not be about your products or services, but about the people who would use those products or services. Not about a hotel in Goa, but challenges of people who go to Goa. Not about your automobile brand, but about people who use cars. Not about your bank, but about people who struggle with personal finance.

'The content must not be about your products or services, but about the people who would use those products or services.'

Not about your cosmetics brand, but about people who care about beauty and wellness. Not about your restaurant, but about people who love food. You get the drift.

Content is about impacting their life, with the brand acting as a facilitator. Obsess about your users, their life and their pain points, not about how big your logo is. Once you start caring about your users, every share you get on your content will take your brand further to reach millions.

At my desk at work, I have pasted, in big bold letters, a sign that reads, 'Nobody gives a f**k about you, your products or services'. It's about your users, their pain points and their well-being. If, through content, we can create a meaningful impact in their lives, we'd have evangelists on our side and not just customers. Every time someone shares your content, it acts as an endorsement; that person approves of what is being said, sharing it with their friends and family, and the brand goes along for a ride without having to aggressively market themselves.

> 'Nobody gives a f**k about you. It's about your users, their pain points and their well-being. If, through content, we can create a meaningful impact in their lives, we'd have evangelists on our side and not just customers.'

IUCTC

I U... What? To streamline the process of generating ideas for share-worthy content, I have filters through which all ideas are passed before we finalize on the one. A short, handy abbreviation I use is IUCTC, where:

I is for Inspirational content,
U is for Useful,
C is for Celebrating their life,
T is for Topical content, and
C is for Change the world.

For me, every brainstorming meeting where ideas are discussed starts with this checklist, and every category on that list is backed by millions of views and is validated by past experiments. It's not that this is written in stone. However, this has given me the best bang for my buck while creating content that went viral in the last few years. It acts as a roadmap, providing a direction for picking killer ideas for content. So let's see what each point entails.

I, for inspirational content

The biggest video which validated this category hit 40 million views in a week, got 1 million shares and added 200K new fans to Ixigo's Facebook page. Inspirational content is often a tall order. It is something that users watch and then feel compelled to share or tag their friends and family in, so they too can be inspired.

What you need to figure out is what kind of content will inspire your users. A very simple video made at Ixigo titled 'Unusual Beaches on Earth' was just a listicle with pictures. To this all the fundamentals discussed in this book were applied, and the video went crazy when it first released in 2016. The 40 million views in a week mentioned above is this video. Sometimes, the biggest results come from the simplest of executions. We scaled up that one video to eight similar videos, totalling 120 million views. It is about finding what kind of content will fascinate and inspire your users, and keep them engaged enough to share with their friends.

When you start brainstorming, the goal must be to hit at least 200 inspirational ideas before you narrow down on the one that seems most exciting. Even if you think you're in a seemingly boring or conventional business category, scratch beneath the surface and you'll find tons of inspirational ideas. Case in point, a video for a restaurant in Hyderabad was just about Hyderabadi dishes to try before you die. That video got 5000 shares across the city and increased footfall by 70 per cent in a week. A friend, who runs a start-up dealing with the buying and selling of cars, started creating content around the fanciest cars and bikes in the world; a wedding planner I met at an event had a light-bulb moment when he discovered he could showcase the most lavish weddings in fast-moving videos. Not just that, a founder of a plus-sized clothing brand soon learnt she could showcase the style of plus-sized celebrities; an app for young parents came up with the idea of showing how successful parents balance work and life; an accounting firm I knew of, came up with ideas for content around the biggest mergers in history and how they happened, and so on.

Inspiring someone is a challenge, but it is the category that has given me the maximum return on minimum investment. All you have to do is curate ideas and weave them into a narrative. Start by making a list of 200 ideas; then choose from that. When you start working on a list of 200 ideas, the first 20 are easy to come up with. What follows is the uphill battle of finding more ideas; here, brainstorming with other people helps a lot. The deeper we dig to find that elusive idea for content, the better our overall video becomes.

U, for useful content

This is, by far, my favourite type of content. When someone watches a video that helps them in some way, they will want to share it with their peer group. The shelf life of such videos is evergreen. Useful ideas for content are born out of pain points, and not just problems. Pain points are the tiny frustrations people face, and in them are hidden micro emotions. When we make an extensive list of pain points, we can then start connecting the dots, and find creative ways to find solutions and showcase them in tiny videos.

Case in point, a video in 2014 called 'Coolest Travel Hacks', went on to become Asia's most-shared branded Facebook post that year (Campaign Asia). The video was about efficient ways to pack your bags when travelling. Building on that momentum, we made another video on hotel hacks, which crossed 30 million views (it was copied extensively by multiple Facebook and YouTube channels) and we even made a few in Hindi, like 'Train *Jugaad*', which hit millions of views and thousands of shares.

The CEO of a British hair-care products brand called me once, to talk about how they could promote their latest hair gel in India. I told him that if they truly wanted a share-worthy video, they should focus on creatively solving a pain point for young men when it comes to their hair. I suggested creating a new kind of helmet for bikers, which keeps their hair intact while still being protective. Every biker knows how wearing a helmet almost always kills their hair style, and that's a pain point no one is addressing. If they could invest in creating a product like that, great, if not, even a product demo video which shows the vision of this new product, could be awesome. Since it's a refreshing take on an age old issue for men, if the idea picked up, people would share this video with their peers with similar pain points and the company would get free coverage.

I was once speaking at an event organized by an online education start-up in Dublin. They wanted to understand how they could create engaging content to promote their online course in nutrition. What started as a list of pain points people had regarding nutrition, became an idea about solving the challenge of awareness around food. The idea was this: what if different types of food showed up at an interview. It would show an interviewer ask the usual interview questions about strengths, weaknesses, five year plan etc. to different types of food items. Imagine a tomato answering questions about its strengths! Now instead of creating boring nutritional content, it would be a fun way to solve the pain points about nutritional awareness in food.

Whatever business you're in, start thinking about how you can solve your customer's tiniest challenges. Start by making a thorough list of their pain points; walk in their shoes, talk to them, figure out what frustrates them, then do some research and see if you can creatively solve these problems. For example, for train travellers, dirty toilets are a pain point. So we made videos with hacks on how to carry soap, making DIY (do it yourself) toilet seat covers at home, even hacks on DIY water jets! I once met the founders of an app that helped young parents, and a simple brainstorming session about the pain points of young parents resulted in a video with 6 million views about remedies for babies when they catch a cold. A food tech start-up got the idea of creating videos called 'One-Minute Breakfast Hacks', as breakfast seemed to be a pain point for many. An automobile company made a video on car hacks, creatively solving most common pain points for car owners; a lingerie brand had already started a bra hacks video last I met them; a fashion brand had planned a video series on one-minute beauty tips, and so on.

If you watch a lot of life hack videos, useless inventions or hacks about every little thing, you can start connecting the dots on how those solutions can apply to your users' pain points, and you will soon have ideas for your own hacks' video.

C, for celebrating their life

When you make an extensive list of pain points, you will soon see there are some you can creatively solve, and those make for useful content, and then there are the ones you cannot; you celebrate these pain points. Creating content that's relatable and celebrates everyday life gives people a sense of shared identity.

In mid-2016, we had to make a video about a hotel in Goa. Now, Goa is already an overly celebrated destination, and brings with it images of parties, beaches, water sports, etc. So, instead of making a video about the hotel or Goa, we focused on the people who go to Goa. We started by creating an extensive list of travellers' pain points when they plan a trip to Goa. The boys had the usual issues – flight costs, renting vehicles, getting in to parties, and so on. The girls, however, had a peculiar pain point – their parents either wouldn't, or were hesitant, to let them go to Goa! So we asked all the guys to leave the room and asked the girls to tell us everything their parents say to them when they wanted to make plans to go to Goa. Within 20 minutes the script was ready. It was a list of bullet points of all the stuff parents say when girls wanted to go on a trip. Now, we couldn't solve this through a video; so the video humorously addressed their situation instead, titling it, 'Things Parents Never Say about a Goa Trip', and it went through the roof! All the comments were by women and they tagged three or four other friends, and it spread like wildfire. We repeated this on Women's Day, by making a video about all the stuff women have to hear when they want to travel (from parents, spouses, and so on). This time it was backed up by a survey to validate the insights. The video called '#RukJanaNahi' went crazy among women!

The goal is to dig deep into the little things, the tiny insights, the micro moments, and celebrate them with content. For example, a video for trains titled 'Train *Mein Hai Ghar Wali Baat*' went on to hit 15 million views, got 100K shares and the Railway Minister of India was inspired to write a little poem, which he shared along with the video. Stuff like this you can't buy; your content must earn it. For the video, an extensive list of pain points was compiled; following which, train trips were taken to validate them, allowing us to add new points along the way. That's how we discovered little details like when people go to use the washroom in a train, they wear whoever's *chappal* is available; how kids always dream of pulling the chain; how food is shared and how advice is freely given without it being asked for!

I was in Goa once, at a marketing conference, in a very expensive hotel. On that trip I kept wondering about all the pain points people have when they stay in hotels, and then my phone buzzed. My wife had just messaged to remind me to bring those shower caps you get for free in hotel bathrooms. Chuckling, I looked around the luxurious property and then at my phone, and thought, no one ever told me about what's okay and not okay to take from hotel rooms. For example, you could take a shower cap, sure, but not a bathrobe. After verifying a long list from friends in the hotel industry, the video titled 'Stuff you can take from hotels' was born. It almost became like a fun educational guide to stuff you cannot take from hotel rooms, and who else would make this, but a travel brand.

So when you make a thorough list of your user's pain points, see which ones you can use to create useful content , and which ones you can celebrate to create relatable content. For example, ideas like 'Five Things Every Mechanic Says', or 'Things Vegetarians are Tired of Hearing', 'Things Moms Hate', 'How Indians Tip in Restaurants', 'Student Life be Like', 'Car Accidents in Delhi vs

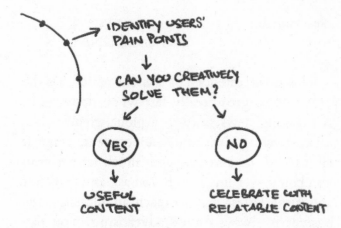

Mumbai', etc. are all very relatable. The bottom line is that by creating relatable content, you bring your brand to the level of a consumer and become a reason for discussions in their peer group. And that keeps you relevant in conversations on social media newsfeeds.

T, for topical content

Topical content is an interesting category. On the one hand, it can get you massive reach, and spread like wildfire; but, on the other hand, its shelf life is short. The fancy word for topical content is 'newsjacking', which simply means we align our brand DNA with breaking news, create content fast and ride the wave of massive public interest in a trending story.

Newsjacking =   Breaking news +
                      Your brand DNA

This is the category of content which has the potential to grow really fast when done right. A breaking news story or a global trend is like a fast-flowing river and your content, when it aligns with its currents, goes much farther than you could ever imagine. If you ask any marketer about the fastest way to reach an audience, the answer is always online advertising. You pay Facebook or Google, for example, and it instantly starts showing your ads to its users, bringing traffic to your website or app. Topical content has that power to instantly reach a big audience and is the only category which can beat online advertising,

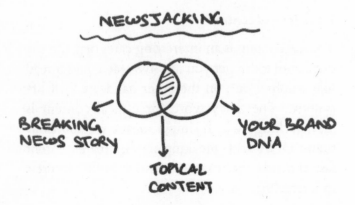

and help your branding without costing your company a bomb.

So the question is, how can you successfully newsjack? From my experience, I like to imagine two circles: One is a breaking news story (Donald Trump winning the US elections, India beating Pakistan in cricket, news regarding the Mars rover, etc.), and the other, is your brand DNA. The area where these two circles intersect is where you have your topical content. When something big happens, our team almost becomes like CNN for two hours; we brainstorm and create content fast, before the trend dies down. For example at Ixigo, topical content ideas were at the intersection of breaking news story and travel. When Trump won the American elections, we created a tiny video showing a man running from the US to Canada; that's it! It hit 300K views within a couple of hours. It helped thousands express their feelings through that little video. And when the 2014 FIFA World Cup went into the final matches, we made a slide deck of funniest FIFA moments (Messi carried Argentina, Neymar carried Brazil, British Airways carried England… You get the drift), which we released on Slideshare, and went on to become the top slide deck, featured on Slideshare's homepage globally.

Topical content helps the brand stay relevant in conversations during any big trend. Sometimes you have to respond in a few hours, other times you can plan in advance. You know certain events will trend on particular days, so put that down on your calendar. April Fools' will trend for a day, and so will Republic Day, Diwali, Dussehra, Christmas, New Year's, etc. By planning, you get more time to draw the two circles and plan your content, which will lie at the intersection. For example every April Fools' Day at Ixigo, we create fake product videos which go viral – from launching executive-class auto rickshaw services (Search for 'Ixigo RickAir'), to smart glasses and smart locks. All the video ideas had our brand DNA (travel), yet they were just pranks for April Fools' Day. Things got so crazy that in 2017, we released a fake pair of smart glasses and it got the CEO an invite to present them at a major Internet conference within fifteen minutes of the video's release! (Search for 'Ixigo Glass', to see the video) For Dussehra, we created a series of images and memes imagining how Ravana would travel in today's day and age (a hotel room with ten pillows, etc.); on Diwali, we created a simple video containing a visual (bought for just $20) showing what India looks like from space on Diwali; for Mother's Day, we created a video which showed an hour of someone's morning routine before a journey with the tagline 'Behind Every Traveller, There Is a Mother', etc.

Inspite of the power of topical content, its shelf life remains a challenge. All the effort which goes into creating topical content is good for one day or one breaking news trend. An April Fools' video won't make sense on April 2, for example. The goal is to be ready for any breaking trend you can align your brand DNA with and create content superfast or plan which of the annual trends you can go after with content or videos.

C, for change the world

I believe that when you create content which attempts to make the world a better place, it gives wings to the little hopes inside people that pushes them to be part of a change. When we do something authentic, it can spark a tiny revolution. The first video I ever made which went viral was in this category ('Gurgaon Toll Surprise'). It was an attempt to make the world a happier place and inspire action, even if the act itself was small. When we align our brand DNA with sincerely doing good to make a difference, the chances of that purpose-driven, heart-felt content aligning with people is that much higher.

Whatever your business or brand, when you know your brand DNA and have a vision for the larger reason you exist, you can align that with a good deed and create content which touches hearts and inspires action. If you blatantly make a PR (public relations) story, or tag it as a CSR (Corporate Social Responsibility) activity, the public will not buy it. For example, I suggested to a friend who runs an automobile business that come Diwali, gift 100 wheelchairs to an old age home and call it 'Gift of Wheels'. It has your brand DNA and it is making a difference in someone's life. He hasn't done it yet, but that video would be a win–win. I remember what folks at IIT Bombay did one April Fools' Day. They dropped fake ₹100 notes around the campus and filmed (from afar) unsuspecting people picking them up. When they picked up the notes, the other side of it read, 'It takes the same effort to pick up litter.'

Brainstorm with your team about aligning your brand DNA with a good deed and you'll be surprised how millions will rally behind you because you're doing something right. Just remember, it must be authentic, with no useless drama, and must demonstrate an idea which can inspire action. You can subtly integrate your brand, in the beginning, ending or top right corner as a watermark; but the video must be in the interest of 'changing the world', not about how cool your brand is. Also, keep in mind that more and more younger people, with strong BS radars, are accessing the Internet today. The more real your content feels, the more it will work. In my experience, authenticity beats everything else here. And if it can start conversations, you've hit the bulls-eye.

Let's cook some ideas

I do this exercise in every masterclass I conduct and the outcome is a list of share-worthy ideas, which are actionable from the get go. You can group together with your team or friends over coffee, and brainstorm. Every idea is welcome; it just needs to pass through the following filters:

- Is it within the brand DNA?
- Does it look like an ad? (Drop it if it does)
- Is it fiction? (Non-fiction is simpler to crack, driven by value and not just entertainment)
- Is it inspirational?
- Is it useful? (Focus on pain points + creatively solve them)
- Does it celebrate their life? (Pain points you can't solve, you celebrate)

- Is it topical?
- Does it attempt to change the world?

In the end, you will be left with a bullet point list of final ideas. Once finalized, every bullet point will have sub-bullet points of finer ideas within it, and every sub-bullet point will have its own sub-bullets of different shots. I have followed this process in all my videos.

I meet a lot of people who confess that creativity isn't their forte, and have left it to agencies and professionals to crack the game. However, I believe that just like intelligence, the more we work on our creativity and hone it, the better we get. For your brain to get into a creative gear, it needs to begin connecting the dots and finding patterns. The more reference points that you have in your head about a certain subject, the more dots you can connect.

Now that you're clear about the focus on creating share-worthy content and how to pick share-worthy topics, the next thing is to figure out how you will bring it together – how you should take your ideas and research, and tie it into building a compelling video. For that we need to understand user behaviour and tailor our content to that. So let's explore how to ensure your video grabs attention within three to six seconds!

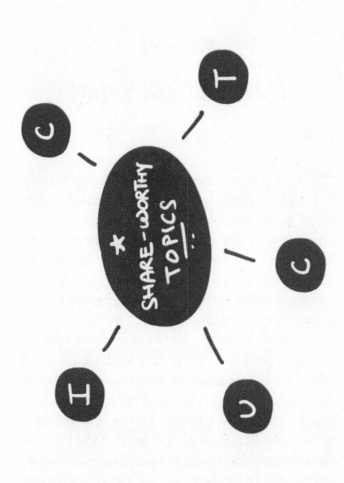

Secret #3

Move Fast and Engage

The average human attention span is only eight seconds long. What this means is that every eight seconds, something happens in our environment that grabs our focus. Our attention keeps hopping from one thing to another all day. Look around, and you see marketing communication everywhere, crying for you to take notice of it. Consider any social media platform. Newsfeeds are chaotic and all content is competing for your attention. Why do you think clickbait (clickbait is a headline or thumbnail link that is designed to lure users to click) has become such a big deal? It is driven by one motive – to get users to stop scrolling through and get them to click on the content! Low attention span is a big challenge, and we need to be very aware of this and tailor our videos and content accordingly. This way we not only gain their attention meaningfully, but deliver

on the promise made in the headline, video title
or thumbnail image as well.

First impressions matter

For any kind of content, the first impression is a
make or break factor. It can amplify the content,
and make sure it gets a lot of engagement, or it
can just kill it.

That's why I love checking news sites every
day. They have been managing first impressions
by way of headlines for their news stories since
forever. The homepage of CNN or NDTV, to
me, is a collection of the best headlines. The more
compelling the headline, the more people are likely
to click on the news story. If you check out a news
site daily, you will notice how they keep changing
the headline for that one story until it gets the
attention it deserves. That's why writing good
headlines is an essential skill for any marketer. Even
in my team, every filmmaker needs to be great
at writing multiple headlines, because apart from
the video title, the copy that goes on Facebook or
Instagram needs to have a separate title that must
be as compelling as the original.

Apart from the headline, the thumbnail of the
video is equally important. The thumbnail is the
image you see of the video before it plays. It needs

to be compelling; it needs to give the user enough reason to engage with the video. Just open YouTube or Facebook and find videos which have millions of views, make a list of 20 of them and see how their thumbnails are designed. It's not rocket science, but once you've gone through 20, you'll know how to put the most compelling message in that thumbnail.

Thumbnail before thumbs up!

The first impression your video makes on the audience is with the thumbnail image. In the entire process of video creation, crafting a compelling thumbnail image should be of top priority. It's like designing the cover of a book; it must be compelling enough for a reader to pick it up in a bookstore, with every other title competing for the reader's attention. For that reason, here are the simple rules I follow for designing thumbnail images for videos:

- Show the most interesting shot or visual from your video in the thumbnail. Just make sure it shows some action or expression that is bound to grab attention.
- Make the best use of colours. Bright colours in your thumbnail have more chances of standing

apart from other videos in newsfeeds or from a list of competing videos.

- Include minimal text to give context. Be mindful that some platforms penalize you if you include too much text on a thumbnail (Facebook, for example, requires you to have text under 20 per cent of the entire image area, else its algorithm limits the reach it gives your video or post).
- Plan to have consistent branding for your thumbnails; so that just by looking at your thumbnail, your audience can spot your video in a sea of content.
- Last, but not the least, experiment and test out different thumbnails to see how they affect engagement.

One thing to remember is that picking thumbnails is different for every platform. YouTube and Facebook give you the option to upload custom thumbnails, so you can design one yourself and upload it with the video. On Instagram, you need to pick from one of the shots of the video itself. WhatsApp, Twitter and LinkedIn pick the first frame of your video as the thumbnail. Ever noticed how when you upload a video on WhatsApp it shows up as a black screen sometimes or as a random image? Next time, put a thumbnail image

DESIGNING THUMBNAILS

- SHOW MOST INTERESTING VISUAL
- USE MINIMAL TEXT
- USE BRIGHT COLOURS
- KEEP EXPERIMENTING AND TESTING
- KEEP BRANDING CONSISTENT

as the first frame and see what happens. Since a video plays at 24 frames per second, the first frame won't even be visible when a user plays the video as it would go by so quickly. But, as a thumbnail, it will get user attention.

The second first impression

So you've rocked the first impression game and have a killer thumbnail, which goes on your video. Now that you have your user's attention, you need to keep them meaningfully engaged for the first three to six seconds. That's the *second* first impression you make. The goal for content must be to stop users as they scroll through their newsfeeds (thanks to a compelling thumbnail), hold their hand and engage them for the first couple of seconds. And hopefully, they will watch the whole video and go on to share it. I work with the assumption that user attention span is only three to six seconds long. For that reason, our content must come to the point really fast.

'Content must come to the point really fast.'

While shooting videos, for example, don't waste time on long shots; no 'presented by' or 'powered by'. Just come straight to the point because no one has all the time in the world to wait for it. In my experience, when creating videos, spend time and attention on developing the first three to six seconds. We have tried many different ways to grab user attention – showing the title instantly with a visual, or showing a visually amazing shot and then showing the title, or not showing the title but having it at the top of the frame the entire time, and playing with the best shots. We need to meaningfully hook the audience to our content quickly, so don't keep your best shots for the 'aha!' moment at the end. No one will reach that point if they never even click on the video in the first place.

For example, in the video titled 'Unusual Beaches on Earth' you'll notice how in the first three to six seconds it shows actual footage of a beach (bought for $20) and then dives into beautiful images of other beaches. The images are not static, but fast moving. In another example, a video we did on Valentine's Day (Ixigo, 'My First Time'), we showed the best shot in the first three seconds. So show that 'money shot' right at the beginning without giving away all of your content. If crafting your thumbnail is important, designing the first three to six seconds is the next crucial step for your video.

Keep 'em engaged

In your thumbnail, your content makes a promise to the user that there's something awesome in store for them if they choose to click on it. And when they click on it, that's when you need to deliver on that promise with context and maintain that quality throughout the video. Content with clickbait sometimes fizzles out after the first few seconds. You'd get your views then, but no shares, and that's when the video will nosedive to a grim death.

The whole game is to meaningfully keep your audience engaged throughout the video. For that, in many of our videos, I follow a 11101010111 principle. Don't worry, this has nothing to do with binary code. It's just that non-fiction content videos (as opposed to fiction) are driven by value and not just a storyline. Say we make a video about 10 things travellers will relate to or 11 themed restaurants in your city. We take the best ideas and assign '1' to awesome or the most interesting shots or points in the narrative, and '0' to what are a little less awesome. When we're editing the video, we align the first three shots or scenes which are excellent (hence 111), and then alternate the 0s and 1s. Show the best in the first 20 per cent of the video and then end with engaging content again, so we get that share.

If you look closely, you'll notice this pattern in the videos I have talked about. The goal is to engage the user in the first three to six seconds and then keep them engaged every six seconds. If you study a graph of a user's watch time for any video, you'll know how it starts with a bang before the curve goes south very quickly. To keep the curve up, we need to make sure that every six seconds we have got something interesting to show.

EDITING NON-FICTION VIDEOS

1 1 1 0 1 0 1

1 = AWESOME SHOT
0 = LESS AWESOME SHOT

Size does matter: Short is king

Among the different formats of video content, the short format is a clear winner. Just like how a snack is had between meals, short-form videos are snacks we consume all day. If you look at all the start-ups getting massively funded in China, for example, they are short-form video apps. And this trend is beginning in India too. Look at the rise of TikTok.

Short videos of one to three minutes are the current rage. They are easy to consume, there's no big commitment from the user to invest their time. I'm not saying longer videos or web series aren't great. The current trend simply happens to be that short formats are grabbing user attention. But you must always experiment with other formats too. If you have a long video, for example, try to cut a short version of it for Facebook or WhatsApp and have a link to the longer video, which lives on YouTube. Most users spend time on Facebook just hanging out and then go to YouTube as a destination to watch videos. So longer videos work for YouTube, where users go with the intent of watching a video, and the shorter form works well for all other social media platforms, where the intent is to hang out, with videos being seen as an added bonus.

From picking topics that are share-worthy to crafting the video, we now need to destroy the myth which comes with the big old world of video production: cost. Let's deep dive into the next chapter, which is all about video production on low budgets. Because for great videos you don't need massive production, just great storytelling.

FIRST
IMPRESSION
(THUMBNAIL
IMAGE)

↑

HOW TO
MOVE FAST
AND ENGAGE

↓

SECOND
'FIRST'
IMPRESSION

(FIRST 3-6
SECONDS)

Secret #4

Storytelling Beats Production Value

The founders of an online video editing app called me one day to ask how they could promote their product and make it reach the millions who wanted to create video content easily. One hurdle they faced when working with both big and small brands was that many clients did not have a video strategy as part of their marketing plan, and needed to be convinced about investing in videos. The founders wondered why this was when video content remained the biggest marketing trend year after year. The reality is that for many companies and chief marketing officers, creating videos is an expensive affair. It is easier for them to produce in-house blog posts than create a video as it would take lakhs of rupees to produce good quality videos if one were to factor the cost of a production house, creative agency, talent, and so on. It was usually deemed too expensive to churn out videos every month. The truth is that it is the agencies that have created this myth that videos require big budgets. One reason this happens is because every agency has dreams of having their ads run on TV; so they think 'TV' when it comes to videos. It is a hangover from the TV era, and many brands and companies still live with the myth that video production is an expensive affair.

'Many brands and companies still live with the myth that video production is an expensive affair.'

I remember the first video which hit millions of views in my journey (Ixigo 'Coolest Travel Hacks'). In terms of reach, it had numbers comparable to the almighty TV. Take a guess at how much we spent to make the video? ₹1500! Another video which beat these numbers and reached 200 million Facebook users ('Unusual Beaches on Earth') was made on a...take a guess... ZERO budget! All the videos I've ever worked on have been made on ridiculously low budgets, but had kick-ass storytelling.

In a video made in January 2018, we experimented with using a celebrity voice-over. We spent 90 per cent of the budget on that one voice-over, and spent the rest on video production, the quality of which we did not compromise on. It hit 15 million views and 100K–plus people shared it. Not just that, in 2019, we produced a rap song (100 per cent in-house), riding the topical wave of hip-hop and rap in the country. Many brands were experimenting with creating rap songs then, and ours was written alongside many big-budget branded songs. Ours was the only one made on an extremely low budget, but competed head-on with the best (Google 'Ixigo Train *mein* Swag' to check it out)!

'How many Bollywood movies have failed because they lacked a good story, even though the special effects were done by Hollywood specialists?'

Gone are the days where you needed a couple of lakhs to produce videos and then crores for distribution on TV. Today, we control the production and distribution. You have the power of an HD camera on your phone, and can edit and share the video online yourself. Many big brands have already started investing in in-house content teams and are churning out content on low budgets regularly. I feel production value is important, but storytelling must take priority over it. How many Bollywood movies have failed because they lacked a good story, even though the special effects were done by Hollywood specialists? The same rules apply for content as well.

It's for a tiny screen!

While creating videos, it must be remembered that everyone is consuming it on their phones. It's that tiny screen we're creating content for. Not for TV, not for movie theatres, but a tiny four- to six-inch screen. And for a tiny screen, massive video production is not necessary. The production value must be determined by where the audience will watch your video – the size of the screen. When you're creating movies, yes, you need to fill a big screen; for TV, sure, the same logic can apply. But for a tiny mobile screen, all you need to do is to keep your

> 'The production value must be determined by where the audience will watch your video, the size of the screen.'

videos clutter-free, visuals front and centre, and fast moving.

I'm not dissing the idea of high-production videos; heck, I love Netflix and their high-production value shows. But it must not act as a deterrent to get you started on your video journey. Our audience has grown up watching a lot of content and it's good storytelling they crave for, more than the camera angles or orgasmic shots filmmakers keep obsessing over. I remember the time I attended a film school for three months. All they taught us was how movies are made in Mumbai with a crew of a hundred people – one person heading every department and specialty. It took me six months to unlearn all that was not relevant to the new format of online videos. Since my first video that went viral ('Gurgaon Toll Surprise'), my entire focus has been on how to make content that works on a tiny screen

'When you're low on resources, you're forced to figure things out by improvising and experimenting.'

effectively, without spending too much on production. And the initial years of being in a start-up helped because a lack of resources is the best motivation to get creative, I've learnt. When you're low on resources you're forced to figure things out by improvising and experimenting. That first video which went viral (while working at Ixigo) was shot entirely on my iPhone and had to be completed by evening because the sunlight coming through the window was the only source of lighting!

Think beyond fiction

One challenge I've faced earlier, and see many dealing with today, is regarding how we think of videos. Growing up, videos to me were movies, TV shows or ads – all of which were fiction. There was always a story – a hero, something that happens and a resolution at the end. I realized early on, however, that for fiction, we need to understand the fine art of telling stories like movie directors do – get actors to portray complex human emotions and create magic on the screen. Also, for fiction we need time to establish characters and context before anything meaningful can happen, which we can't afford when user attention span is so short. So when it came to creating content, I dumped the idea of fiction (which was also very competitive) and focused entirely on the value the video would provide to users. I decided to experiment with non-fiction instead, which was largely unexplored, and pump it with creativity. Creativity can also be in curation, not necessarily creation. You could make a list of, say, 10 things which could help your users, and visualize that as a fun, entertaining video. All you would need for that is to research on Google, make a list of points, then create a list of shots you will need and stitch them together. When you

> **'Creativity can also be in curation, not necessarily creation.'**

do this 20 times, you get better at researching, finding new ideas and visually representing it in a video.

I've always believed that creativity can be structured and nurtured, and when we create content based entirely on value, all we need is solid research. When we dig deep to understand our users, make extensive lists of creative solutions or relatable frustrations, and watch a lot of other videos for visualization examples, we start to connect the dots. That's when an original idea, and a way to visualize it, is born. For example, if you've never heard Indian classical music, how can you ever imagine or appreciate fusion music? You need experiences to connect the dots. While doing workshops with start-ups and big brands, this exercise has yielded killer ideas, all born out of simple process.

Hack for fiction

As I continue to experiment with fictional content, I stick to a method to help make it easier to execute and remember all the elements required. I learnt this in my film school days and, whenever I get lost in the subjective creativity of how a fictional story should proceed, I apply this hack. It's about breaking down the story into three steps – C.A.R.

C for context or conflict,
A for action, and
R for resolution

You can explain any movie with this concept. There's a character who faces conflict, or we set the character in a particular context. Then the character takes action to solve that conflict or deal with the situation. The ending is the resolution; the win at the finish. Movies spread this over two hours, but when I think up a two-minute video, this concept works like magic. It provides a simple framework to tell stories. It's not that this is the best method or that there aren't other concepts, but I find this easy to focus on and execute. We're creating two–three minute content videos, and the more our focus is on curating an idea and a simple process for execution, the better our chances of success without having to spend a bomb. Picking the right idea is the key. The more authentic it is, the less ads-y it is, the more shareable it will be.

The hack for low-cost production

If you want to create low-budget videos, you will need to take control of the project, not outsource it completely, and learn how to improvise. The way to cut costs in video production is to take charge of the creative process: the idea and how it should be executed. You don't have to become Spielberg to figure this out; all you need is to research ideas and the ways they could be visually presented. When you take the bulk of creativity out of the equation, then even if you hire freelancers to shoot and edit, they just execute your vision and it costs less. You can find skilled filmmakers (there are tons of photography groups on Facebook) willing to build their portfolio or student filmmakers who are passionate and fast learners. I'm not saying exploit them by paying less, but find a win–win solution. Alternatively, you can hire experienced folk; but hire them for an entire day, so you can churn out more in that time. Also, a working relationship with them will help you build an in-house team, eventually.

So, once you have identified ideas based on the process I shared in the chapter about picking topics, you must be sure to give the team proper direction. Decide how you want the project to turn out, or else they can make a Qutub Minar when you ordered a Taj Mahal. The strategy is to give them an idea for a video and then a 'sensibility reference', so they know how that idea should look visually. For example, say you identified your users' pain points and decided to create a 'hacks' video, which creatively solves those pain points. Attach with that a 'sensibility reference' of, say, a BuzzFeed-type video or any video you love, for how the video must look visually. Now, the team has a clear direction of the concept and something to compare their execution to. Even if they mess it up, it would be 60–70 per cent close to the reference video. If you're planning to have an in-house team, I say hire student filmmakers, and groom them by asking them to blatantly copy 10 videos with the sensibility you like. Ask them to copy it frame by frame and recreate the thing. But do not release these videos! By copying 10 videos and learning to overcome their shortcomings with every attempt, they will build on their skills. The 11th video will be much better in execution and they will be ready to execute an original idea.

The bullet point way of writing screenplays easily

One thing I obsess about is how we write the script and screenplay for a video. I chucked the traditional approach of writing screenplays since I wanted it to be a simpler process. I started training teams to start creating videos, with the points I had picked up, on their own. Since the human attention span is so short, every few seconds something new must happen on-screen to keep users meaningfully engaged. So we created bullet points of all the ideas we had, then wrote down shots for those ideas and tied them all together. Every video must be entertaining, but the bullet-point list ensures we're focused on providing value, and the way we present it is what makes it entertaining.

BEHIND THE SCENES

'Inside the bag of an Indian student going abroad' (2015)

While brainstorming ideas which celebrate users' life, we were focused on celebrating micro moments of Indian travellers. Hunting for ideas on Google, we came a across a blog post that contained data from the TSA (Transportation Security Administration [U.S. federal agency]) about all the things Indians carry in their bags when they go abroad. A simple looking blog post without any major engagement; yet we saw it as an amazing visual narrative because it, in a tiny way, expresses who we are as Indians. So we dug deeper, researched across flight-, airport- and aviation-related blogs from around the world, mined Quora and, in the end, we had an extensive list of the items Indians students carry when they go abroad. It was just a bullet-point list of items. We finalized the most interesting ones and we had a great idea for a video. The bullet-point list of all items Indians students carry set a clear direction for the video. It had items like pressure cookers, Maggi, medicines, a tabla, etc. We went to a nearby market and got all the stuff. Renting a pressure cooker was an interesting experience; the shop owner couldn't understand why we needed to rent a utensil! We spent less than ₹2000 on all the items. Now we had a bullet-point list of items. Next, we made sub-bullet points below each point about how we would show each item. So the bullet-point list started becoming a screenplay, because we had listed multiple ways to shoot and visualize every item. Once that was ready, we shot the video. One of the meeting rooms in the office had wooden flooring. We placed a table with a chair on top of it, and tied the camera and tripod on top of the chair, so the camera faced downwards to provide us with a crisp wooden background, and we shot the video as per our bullet-point list. We bought footage worth $20 of an actual bag at an airport and put it in the beginning of the video with the title for context. The video hit a million views in the first week, and was picked up by NDTV and showcased on their front page under the 'offbeat' section. In a few weeks, it climbed to 5 million views, and today, it's still hovering on newsfeeds at 8 million views.

It's called motion pictures for a reason

One thing I learnt early on was that when it comes to movies or videos, it's all about the visual storytelling. So I edited videos (back when I was attending filmmaking classes) with the sound switched off initially. The idea was that the video must make sense visually first. Try watching any foreign-language film and few minutes into it, you'll realize that you can grasp the story even without understanding the dialogues. This little practice has helped out as Facebook, Instagram and even LinkedIn now autoplay videos in newsfeeds, with the sound switched off. Execute visual storytelling first, then work on sound, and make sure you put big and bold subtitles (if you have spoken words in the video). For one, everyone will be watching it on their tiny phones (hence, the need for big subtitles) and they will continue watching your video even if they are unable to play it with sound. Making 'sound-proof' videos helps in nailing the visual storytelling before you do anything else.

'Making "sound-proof" videos helps in nailing the visual storytelling before you do anything else.'

Lights, camera...action

When it comes to the basics of video production, I believe in applying common sense and making use of what is easily available around you. Lighting is important for a video, so whatever the subject of your shot (person or an object), make sure it's well lit. You can shoot in the sunlight, or next to a window, use your office or house lights in a way that the subject is well lit. All you have to do is ensure it looks neat, clean and clutter-free on a tiny screen. We've made so many videos using natural light from the window and they have all hit millions of views. As I mentioned earlier, production value must be determined by where the video will be played. If the videos will be played on tiny screens, all you have to do is make sure your frame is well lit. We put a yellow chart paper on the table for the background and shot near the window for a few videos. When we checked how it looked on the phone, we saw that it worked beautifully. You can invest in buying a set of lights if you're setting up an in-house team, but always operate from common sense before you get into the technicalities. It's not rocket science to see if the subject is well lit or not, or if the shot looks good on a tiny screen or not.

When it comes to the camera, the HD camera on your phone is good enough to get started. I bought a DSLR primarily for the feature that helped blur the background, which made the frame look more crisp and clean. I learnt later it was called 'depth of field', but, at that point, it was just me applying common sense to the situation. My goal was not to become a professional videographer, but to apply the equipment to fulfil my needs, and focus on storytelling. For a tiny screen, you don't need massive equipment. You can invest in better equipment, sure, but to get started, you need to practice your storytelling first and, with basic equipment, you can still get great results. Of course a better camera or sound recorders will enhance the whole video, but it should not stop you from getting started.

> 'You can invest in better equipment, sure, but to get started, you need to practice your storytelling first and, with basic equipment, you can still get great results.'

In the past five years, we've used phone cameras, DSLRs, drones, and even expensive movie cameras, all in the name of experimentation. If we're making a video which may play on TV, we invest in the bigger cameras and crew; if it will play on social media platforms, we work with basic DSLRs or our phones; if you're thinking of making video blogs, stick to your phone cameras to get started and upgrade to DSLRs once you have a handle on your narrative, like most video bloggers do. The whole point is that it's never about the equipment.

If you love the idea of learning and working with high-tech equipment, great! But, if you ask any great photographer or filmmaker, they'll tell you that it's not about how you shoot, but what you shoot. Fancy cameras or equipment may increase the value

'It's not about how you shoot, but what you shoot.'

of production, but if you learn to focus on the need, you will eventually use only what is needed to fulfil that requirement.

Whenever we're working on a video, just before the shoot I have a meeting with the team about equipment. We have endless budget discussions (since we never spend like crazy) and determine what equipment we require based on the need of the project. If we're shooting in-house, we just use the DSLR we have; if it's an outdoor/guerrilla shoot, we rent DSLRs, which would work better there (look for DSLR rental companies in your city). Our meetings are never about what the budget is; rather, we talk about what we need and then we set the budget. I hate when the first question production houses or ad agencies ask, when you approach them for a project, is, 'What's your budget?' Forget the budget, tell me what you need to achieve the vision, then give me options.

That's why we choose to do a lot of our videos in-house; it gives us more control, and allows us to keep a tight watch on how the money is spent.

For sound, if it's dialogue or spoken word, we either use the voice recorder on the iPhone or record it on ZOOM H1 (a basic voice recorder you can buy), and then match the footage with the sound in the editing stage. Sometimes, it's also a good idea to book a sound recording studio; they aren't expensive, they charge by the hour and you can easily find one in your city. We buy background scores from stock music sites (like pond5.com or the plethora of stock music sites on the Internet). We download 10 different sound files, test them out, buy whatever works best, and add it to the video.

For editing, you can try the basic editing software which comes on a Mac or a Windows computer to begin with. When starting out, all you need is to put different shots together; nothing fancy. Remember, the whole exercise is about lining up different shots to make into one whole narrative in the end. iMovie or Windows Movie Maker does that quite easily. When you start making more videos, you can get Final Cut Pro or Adobe Premiere Pro, or any editing software for a more advanced and sharper edit. When you get to the advanced stage, you can use these softwares for colour correction and colour grading too (which makes the video look crisp), but that comes later when you're getting better at visual storytelling and need a little more finesse.

You can also try experimenting with different apps and websites that offer easy-to-use tools to create videos. My favourite on the iPhone is Clips and iMovie (both by Apple), which help me shoot and edit directly on my phone. It works well for video blogs. You can search and find an abundance of video apps for iOS or Android that can help you produce videos. There are also the drag-and-drop variety of video apps like Typito, Lumen5 or Rocketium. They make videos for all dimensions (square, vertical, etc.), work in the sound and move pictures effortlessly. Now, if the person who writes blog posts starts using drag and drop apps like these, every article can soon be visualized with a tiny video.

Always remember

In the end, it's not about which tools you use, but what you're trying to show. Tools and equipment are easy to get; figuring out what you want to show is the big task ahead of you. I remember, back in the day, I taught myself how to use Final Cut Pro in a week, and then edited the video I was working on. Even while hiring a team, I'm looking for individuals who invest their time in self-development and learning. It isn't a big deal to learn new tools or software. What's really important is the direction in which you fire your bazooka!

Secret #5

Make for Mobile

It's a no-brainer that mobile usage has surpassed desktop computers in the last few years. A *Times of India* article in 2018 reported that of all the time we spent on the Internet in 2017, 90 per cent was spent on a mobile phone!* India almost tops the list of nations when it comes to using Internet on mobile devices. All across the country, and the world, the online experience has shrunk to a tiny screen. And when everyone is spending a crazy amount of time every day on their phones, it makes sense to tailor your content to a tiny screen.

There has been a massive shift in user behaviour when it comes to consuming content. From the days of the desktop computer being a luxury, the mobile phone has become a necessity for the

---

* Shalina Pillai, 'We use 90 per cent of online time on the phone', *Times of India*, 20 April 2018.

masses. The '*roti, kapda aur makaan*' slogan from the 1970s has now become '*roti, kapda, makaan aur Internet*'. When we're creating content, I'm always mindful of where the content will be consumed and if the experience is made for a tiny screen. The content should, first, be easy to access, and, second, be easy to share. It's all about the composition of our visual content, imagined and calibrated for a four- to six-inch screen. For traditional filmmakers, this was a big challenge to overcome, adapting big screen storytelling to a screen in a pocket.

> **'When everyone is spending a crazy amount of time every day on their phones, it makes sense to tailor your content to a tiny screen.'**

From rectangle to square

Videos have always been rectangular in their shape and size. Aspect ratio (the ratio of the width to the height of an image or a screen) for videos was always 4:3 or 16:9. And it is a rectangle because movie screens have always been rectangular, TV screens have been rectangular, and videos and films have been adapted so they can be shown on large and small rectangular screens. But when it comes to consuming video content on mobile phones, we tend to use phones vertically. Any video which is made for a rectangle (the traditional) screen will look tiny on a vertically held mobile phone, unless you tilt your phone and unlock the side screen lock. Vine and Instagram started the trend of square videos, but it was Facebook and WhatsApp that really brought this format to the mainstream.

A square video takes up more real estate on a tiny phone screen, when held vertically, and it is effortless to view and share. It hit me one night, at 2 in the morning, as I was busy swiping through videos on Facebook, that square videos were so effortless to view on a mobile phone. Folks in the film industry often get agitated when videos are shot in vertical mode. I was almost shouted at by the instructor in my three-month film school programme because

'Square videos with an aspect ratio of 1:1 take up 78 per cent more real estate in a person's mobile newsfeed than a landscape video, with an aspect ratio of 16:9.'

he kept insisting that a movie must never be shot in vertical mode. But, hey, who cares about what filmmakers and traditional movie makers think when everyone uses their phones vertically and millions consume video content on their phones?

Square vs vertical

Note that there is a difference between a square video and a fully vertical video. A fully vertical video takes up the whole screen, and is a very immersive experience (many video sharing apps are riding on this trend, even Instagram launched IGTV, which is a full vertical video app experience). For one, it's made for a native mobile watching experience. But I feel square videos are easy to view and give one a sense of control of the screen, unlike fully vertical videos, which take up your whole screen. For social media, square content was clearly the winner in all the experiments we did with video sizes. Square videos with an aspect ratio of 1:1 take up 78 per cent more real estate in a person's mobile newsfeed than a landscape video, with an aspect ratio of 16:9. Look at all the viral memes, pictures or videos – a square frame is easy to view (it occupies more screen space on the phone) and is easy to share. On Facebook, for example, the share, comment options are right below the video, and people are more likely to hit them when their phone is on portrait mode because of the ease with which they can type sentences out.

Think for a tiny screen

Now making content for a tiny screen does not mean you create videos for TV and then just release them on YouTube or Facebook. We need to understand that it must be a clutter-free experience for a tiny screen. Look at Facebook, if you add too much text on your images, Facebook penalizes you when you want to boost it (boost is Facebook's word for paying money to show your content to your targeted audience, available to page administrators) because it clutters the screen and spoils the user experience on a tiny screen. Test it out yourself. Take two images, one with text less than 20 per cent of the area and one with more text. You will see how the post with more text gets a warning when you boost it. Pull out pictures from the last vacation you took, make a collage and upload it; then pick a single photo from your trip and upload that too. See which one gets more engagement organically. Facebook and every other social media platform understands that images or any visual content which has clutter spoils their user experience (and poses the threat of having users jump to other platforms). So their algorithms detect such posts and minimize their reach. Platforms have monetized how you reach your audience with your content, killing organic reach, and the way to get the best bang for your 'boost dollars' is to have clutter-free visuals with minimal text. This applies to image posts and thumbnails for videos, but not to the content inside the video.

'Create a clutter-free experience for a tiny screen.'

Rule of the selfie

Now, for a tiny screen, the visuals must be clutter-free, and must be front and centre. Why do you think the 'selfie' has become such a big trend in the last decade? You're at a beautiful beach; to hell with the view! Here's my face up close. It occurred to me one day, while reading a book on photography, that the traditional 'rule of the third' doesn't apply to new-age content any more. The 'rule of the third' says that you keep your subject in one-third of the frame, and the background in the rest. But in a fast-moving, mobile, square-content world, I propose a new rule – the 'rule of the selfie'. Create content like it's a selfie – front and centre! In all the videos we've made, I'm very mindful that the subject of the shot must be front and centre, clearly visible with enough margins. This is the reason I'm a fan of fast action and close-ups in videos. The selfie shooting method, if I can call it that, brings the storytelling front and centre, and looks directly in the eye of the user, just like a selfie does. I hate it when I see videos with tiny subtitles or tiny fonts in them. You expect us to pinch and zoom in to understand the content? It must be effortless to consume the content; so big fonts, big subtitles (strongly suggested if you have a voice-over or dialogues) and clear visuals are absolute necessities now.

VIDEO COMPOSITION

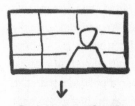

↓   ↓

RULE OF THIRDS (SUBJECT IN 1/3 OF SCREEN)   RULE OF SELFIE (SUBJECT FRONT AND CENTER)

BEHIND THE SCENES

'How to Travel Visa-Free' (2014)

A few years ago, to get ideas for creating content videos, I looked at top-performing blog posts. The one with most engagement contained a list of countries where you could travel visa-free as an Indian. It had thousands of shares and comments – a validation that this content could work as a video. The challenge was to visualize the list as a video. Since mobile-native content was becoming a trend, we decided to make content specifically for the mobile. All we did was get couple of multi-coloured chart papers from a nearby stationery store, a globe, a map and a marker. The video, titled 'Ixigo How to Travel Visa-Free', was shot on an iPhone, with the globe front and centre, and the vibrant chart papers appearing in the background. The whole video was about travelling to countries that are visa-free for an Indian passport holder. We shifted the frames between a globe, a map and even Google Maps on my phone, so the video stays fast moving and doesn't get monotonous. We added fast, quirky music, which we bought off a stock music website and the video was ready. It started getting massive organic engagement and when a politician shared it, it went to another level. That was my first experiment in purposefully creating content for a tiny screen, keeping it clutter-free by using more close shots than long shots, big text and zooming in for an immersive mobile video experience. It wasn't a square video because the square revolution hadn't hit yet. Yet, even in a rectangle form, it was made for mobile.

Not just for videos, for all content

Mobile-native content isn't a concept just for videos, but applies to all types of content. Look at how listicles have become so popular – easy to consume lists, instead of long articles. '10 things about' this, or 'nine things about' that. Look at any long news article on a popular news site and see how they carefully craft their entire article, such that it's easy to consume on a tiny screen. Gone are the days of desktop publishing and infographics. Now, even if you have a long infographic, you need to tailor it to a tiny mobile screen, perhaps cut it into multiple square images that are swipeable. Look at

'Now, even if you have a long infographic, you need to tailor it to a tiny mobile screen, perhaps cut it into multiple square images that are swipeable.'

Slideshare and how the most popular slide decks are the ones that are clutter-free, which keep you swiping for the next slide.

How would they see it?

So the next time you're planning to create any type of content, ask yourself, 'How would the users see it?' Whenever we're editing videos, we never check it on big screens and instead, scale it down to the size of a mobile screen and then take decisions. Even for sound, we test it on multiple mobile devices to see what the experience is like. Be it a blog post you're writing (which in responsive design will adapt to a tiny screen), a meme you're creating or a short video you're shooting, always test it on a mobile screen. What looks great on a big desktop screen may look like rubbish on a tiny screen. My pet peeve is the subtitles. A great video, but tiny subtitles ruin the experience. They look okay on a desktop, but when it comes to mobile viewing you're really asking for too much from your users. Just add subtitles big and bold, and see the magic happen.

MAKE FOR MOBILE ⭐

- KEEP VISUALS CLUTTER-FREE
- APPLY RULE OF THE SELFIE
- FOR ALL TYPES OF CONTENT
- CREATE FOR A TINY SCREEN
- ALWAYS TEST ON MOBILE SCREENS

Secret #6

Think Conversations Before Campaigns

If you look at how marketing and advertising has evolved over the last 100 years, you'd see how the game has changed from being a one-way street to a two-way street for brand communication.

THEN	NOW

ONE WAY (THEY BROADCASTED, WE CONSUMED)	TWO WAY (THEY BROADCAST, WE PARTICIPATE)

Say, it's the 1920s. A Mr Singh has decided to setup a business of selling refreshing beverages. He bottled the drinks in bottles washed at home, and went out on his bicycle to sell his beverages. He realized that to sell more bottles he needed to be where the customers are, where he'd be a solution to their problems. So he picked a busy road, which saw a lot of people rushing to work. He got a table and neatly stacked his bottles. One customer stopped by, and then a few more. Business started rolling; now, he needed help from his family to bottle more beverages at home, to sell them every day. To expand his business, he learnt that he needed more visibility, more people had to see what he had to offer. So he erected a big billboard, and put up a sign about his refreshing drinks, calling them a 'thirst solution'. It worked; people saw it, more customers started stopping by, and his tiny business began to flourish. In a few months, to push sales up further, he scaled up his little operation. Now he put up billboards in five different locations across the city, and rented a warehouse where he could bottle his drinks. The billboard attracted even more customers and his little production unit in the warehouse supplied the products.

Around 1960, Mr Singh passed away, and his son, Ramesh, took over the reins of the business.

Learning from his father, he erected even more billboards across the city, set up a bottling factory, bought shops and assigned distributors. He realized the importance of building a brand and ordered a local painter to create a logo for his brand. He learnt that the bigger his brand, the more orders he'd get from his loyal customer base. Ramesh realized he needed a wider reach, perhaps in nearby cities too. Newspapers and radio were the main means of communication; a lot of people had access to these. It made business sense to be visible where his customers' attention was; so he started advertising in local newspapers and played his ads on the radio, while continuing the billboards that had worked since his father's time. His understanding of advertising was to build a strong recall value for his brand. And, if everyone was hooked to reading newspapers and listening to the radio, that's where his brand had to be – heard and seen, again and again. The more his brand was seen, the more the recall value, and the more products would get sold. The plan worked; more people from nearby cities started buying his products. Business was booming. Ramesh now eyed expanding the business across states, dreaming of a nationwide presence.

It was the mid–1980s, and TV was the new rage; the whole country was hooked to it. It was where the eyeballs were; TV was like the new billboard. By expanding his production to factories, TV ads start rolling out, building Ramesh's brand across the country. It was only a matter of time before orders for his beverages started coming in from around the country. Ramesh had tasted true success – the business that his father had started, with good production and strong advertising, was now booming. He advertised on billboards, in newspapers, on the radio and now, on TV. Celebrities were hired to keep the audience engaged with the ads, while factories churned out bottles by the million.

In 1999, Ramesh died, and his son, Raj, took over the business. Well trained in the family business and savvy about the changing trends, Raj was a sharp Generation X man. He knew the Internet was the next big thing. So he got a website made, all the products were listed on it, just like the earlier times, and customers were told what to buy. Search engines became popular, and websites were soon ranked. So, he spent time optimizing his website with keywords, to ensure he ranked high when the nation wanted a beverage.

Then the Internet exploded, from websites to social media networks. The marketing and advertising fundamentals his grandfather's business had relied on so heavily, were about to be disrupted. User behaviour of the masses started evolving from consuming traditional media to consuming content on social media. Slowly, the control of the media moved into the hands of the masses. Customers now started posting their stories, pictures, and even videos. The one-way communication suddenly became two way. A customer from a small town found an insect in a sealed bottle sold by Raj's brand. That video went viral, it was shared millions of times, and the reputation so carefully built by his grandfather was now at stake. Gone were the days of simply repeating one message over and over again on TV; this was a new world where customers got back to you, engaged with the brand and had the power to build it or destroy it. Competition became fierce and sales started declining. The game had changed. Social media had changed everything.

You can imagine the above story in the case of any traditional business or brand, from Coca-Cola to Parle-G. Social media used to be an option for marketers and advertisers back in the day; now it's something they have to deal with on a daily basis. Remember how the Maggi noodles fiasco exploded on the Internet? Or the isolated case of Amul milk gone sour? Every brand's communication today is judged on the Internet – from a CEO's remarks to isolated product defects. Heck, Snapchat's founder made a remark about India and thousands deleted the Snapdeal app, mistaking it to be Snapchat, from their phones.

Branding today is about relevance, not just recall value

The fundamentals of building a brand have evolved, because user behaviour has evolved. Building recall value for your brand was all about the number of 'eyeballs' you could grab and how many times you could grab them; this way customers remembered your brand when they needed to. With social media changing the media landscape, traditional one-way communication has died. Building brands in this age is about engaging with your customers, and not just swamping them with your message. The goal for

'Gone are the days of bombarding customers' eyeballs and expecting results. The game today is about reaching their hearts and getting authentic engagement.'

branding today is to stay relevant (in conversations on social media), and not just build recall value. Gone are the days of bombarding customers' eyeballs and expecting results. The game today is about reaching their hearts and getting authentic engagement. Several brands are merely yelling in a bid to grab attention, not factoring in the drop in attention span and the increased chaos in users' lives. Now, if you want them to remember you, you need to engage with them, and not just shout at them.

Understanding how social media works for business

Imagine being invited to an event for business, and when you reach you see a massive door blocking your path. You move forward and push it open. What you see inside is the world's biggest party. Millions of people are hanging out and having a good time. There are little parties happening within this giant party. Everyone is talking and mingling with each other. In one corner, the latest movies are being discussed, while a conversation on politics is underway over at the other end. Some groups are discussing parenting issues, others are discussing their careers. Every imaginable conversation is happening somewhere. You are there strictly for business and to find opportunities to market your company. Now, what would happen if you were to pull out your business cards and start distributing them to every discussion you spot? You'd be given looks, then stares and eventually you would be ignored. You're not adding anything of value to their discussions; you are just peddling your company.

This is how social media works. It's the world's biggest party and everyone is having conversations, sharing stories and is busy interacting with one another. To attract people without being too obvious about it, you could put up your own little tent and invite people to conversations; conversations where your company has some relevance. You create content which sparks those discussions, and then seed that content in other groups, hoping that people would come to your tent to continue those conversations. Your brand becomes the channel to start meaningful discussions around your area of business – about problems, issues and pain points of users – and a reminder that your company provides a solution for the issues discussed. The goal is to stay relevant in users' lives. And that's the goal for your content: to start conversations before you plan any campaigns. Your business must matter for your audience, for your users. Because we don't need customers; we

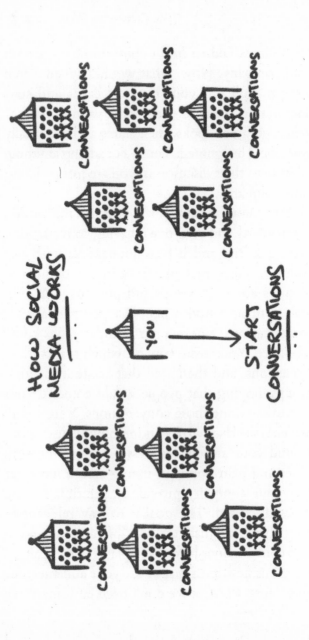

need evangelists who will take those conversations forward and bring others to your brand.

Conversations save you millions in distribution

When your users start engaging with your content, tag their friends and begin comment threads, social media platforms will start loving your content. Facebook, for example, has tightened the screws on their newsfeeds. In the last algorithm update, branded or promotional content has become expensive and gets low visibility on newsfeeds, despite you spending money on it and boosting it. Content shared by friends and family gets priority. Now, if you share content that is in the interest of users, and seed it either organically or by boosting (which I'll cover in the next chapter), the more conversations and engagement it attracts, the lower your cost of distribution will be. Further, Facebook sees that as a signal – it sees that users are engaging more with their friends and family, and since social media platforms cannot control the content users share, your content for the brand can start flying higher on the newsfeeds and staying relevant longer, without your company having to spend a bomb. Great content that starts conversations stays on newsfeeds longer and gets more reach, giving you most bang for your buck.

Handling crisis in conversations

Conversations are not in your hand for they are the outcome of how users perceive your content or communication. When you create and share content, which is authentic and which attempts to meaningfully impact people, the conversations can be aligned with what you had planned. But sometimes, if you're not careful about your content, you can start the wrong kind of conversations, or someone else can start a conversation (beyond your control) which hurts your brand. Dealing with negative conversations on social media can be a daunting task if you're a brand. You can no longer pretend it's a one-way medium. This is a two-way street, and you will have to deal with it. In my experience, the best way to deal with a big crisis, or even a negative tweet or comment, is to plan around defusing it. If it's a negative tweet or a comment, diffuse it with humour; if it's a big crisis respond with a clear clarification or an apology if you're the one at fault.

One question to ask before planning a campaign

Every year more and more campaigns are coming out on every little occasion. Mother's Day, Father's Day, Dussehra, Diwali, Christmas, New

Year's, Friendship Day, Yoga Day, Republic Day, Independence Day, Women's Day, and so many more. Every big or small occasion has become a reason to plan a brand campaign. But there's only one question to be asked here: 'What conversation will it start?'

If your campaign starts the right conversations, you will gain a lot in earned media (when journalists and bloggers start writing about it) through organic reach – with your content going viral for the right reasons – and you'll get a call from your CEO or investors about that pending annual bonus! The five categories of content that I shared in the earlier chapter (Inspirational, Useful, Celebrate their life, Topical or Change the world) help me focus on conversations and form a filter when we're brainstorming ideas. It's not that you have to plan campaigns around occasions only. You can start conversations with your content, completely agnostic of trending topics, and still kill it.

Many of the videos we've done till now have generated immense engagement. A video about unusual beaches led to 400K comments being posted on that single video; a video about Goa trips started a conversation about how group plans always seem to fall through (and it received 40,000 comments). We've done campaigns around

Republic Day, which started conversations of our memories of train journeys; on Women's Day, we started a conversation about how Indian women needed to seek permission to travel; Mother's Day was all about thanking our moms; and April Fools' Day was about ridiculous, fun discussions. We created a series of videos about learning a language, and those videos attracted 23 million views and lakhs of shares and comments. It was not topical, but it started conversations where everyone who watched and shared the video tagged their co-workers, spouses or friends, to introduce their culture through that video. A food video we made for a hotel in Hyderabad started a conversation around haleem, another titled 'Inside the Bag of Indian Students Going Abroad' got thousands of comments from Indians who travel worldwide.

Once you're aware of the conversations your content will start, the biggest task becomes putting your content in front of users. The next chapter is about distribution, how you can catapult your content. If it has wings, it will fly.

Secret #7

Distribution Is Everything

When it comes to content, half the battle is creating share-worthy content that engages the audience, which compels them to take action and share it with others. The other half is to make sure our hard work actually reaches them. One thing I realized, quite early on in the game, was the importance of effective distribution. Without a proper distribution strategy, the best of your videos or content may simply die in a vault. Imagine having worked hard all your life to develop your singing talent. You did everything from taking singing lessons to practising endlessly for hours. One day, you are ready to show the world your talent, only to find that there is no one present to hear you sing, nor is there anyone interested in what you have to offer. Imagine you made the world's greatest movie, but did not have a proper plan in place to distribute it to cinema screens across the country. Great content needs a distribution plan; without that we're just hoping to get found.

'Great content needs a distribution plan; without that we're just hoping to get found.'

Every time a video is released, I become obsessed with my checklist of tasks related to distribution. Once your content is in place, it is equally important to have a distribution plan ready. The goal is, of course, for your content to go viral so that it reaches more and more people, like a snowball hurtling down a mountain, and gets you free distribution in the long run. But, before it snowballs, the content must first reach users. If it doesn't, then it's just another bubble in the water, lost in an instant.

First things first

When your video is ready for release, the first thing is getting it ready for different platforms. I suggest native uploads on each platform, instead of just uploading it on YouTube and then pasting the link everywhere. By this I mean, have multiple versions of your video ready for each platform you're planning to upload it on. Every social media platform today has become a video distributor. When you post a YouTube link on, say, Facebook or LinkedIn, in my experience, the competing video platform doesn't amplify the link, and instead prefers a natively uploaded video. A native video is like posting a picture on Facebook, Twitter, LinkedIn, etc., by uploading the picture directly on each platform, instead of sharing a single link on various platforms. I have seen native video uploads getting far more reach on platforms, compared to, say, YouTube video links. Try it today – take any video, upload it to

YouTube and then share that link in a post on LinkedIn. The next day, upload the video directly as a post on LinkedIn. After two days, compare the views and engagement on both posts, and you'll see the difference.

Also, when posting native videos, make sure you have the right thumbnail. YouTube, Facebook and Instagram give you an option to select the thumbnail, while WhatsApp, Twitter and LinkedIn usually pick the first frame of the video. These platforms are notorious for changing their formats and features; so make sure you Google what their latest video specifications are. You will find tons of articles about any feature change on social media blogs. Once that is sorted, prepare different versions of the text that will be posted with the video on every platform. This step ensures your video caters to each platform individually and is native to that platform. Once this is done, your content is ready to be blasted into the universe; all we need to figure out is when to launch it.

The million views question: When to launch?

In the early days, I could never figure out when to release a video; what day or time was the best to ensure it got a great kick off? Email marketing had taught me to send mails on Tuesdays or Wednesdays, since on Mondays users would be occupied with work, and were unlikely to check promotional emails. By Tuesday or Wednesday, however, people were more likely to open emails not related to work. But that logic didn't seem to make sense when it came to content and videos, because everyone watches videos and consumes content all the time. Facebook, for example, shows you the days and times your users are online (in the Facebook page admin section), and you can see how it's active almost all the time, except late at night, when activity usually dips.

For me, insights gained from experiments were far more important than *gyaan* from countless articles on marketing. In my experience, many of the videos picked up right after midnight, while others did well no matter when we released them (whenever the video was ready). After making numerous videos and hitting millions of views many times, the insight dawned on me: it's all about the initial kick off.

The initial kick off is crucial if you are seeking organic success for your video. It also provides validation to see if your video is worth spending money on, for boosting and promotion. For content that is share-worthy, the benchmark I follow is that it must get 100 shares in the first 10 minutes. Those 100 shares are the most crucial, I've realized. It's like metaphorically kicking your video as hard as you can into the universe. If it has wings, it will take flight and travel to galaxies you didn't even imagine. The first 100 shares will likely come from your immediate community, your organization, friends or family. Whenever it is most convenient for your immediate community to share your video, should determine the time you release the video on the Internet. For example, everyone in my office is relatively free right after lunch or just before the end of the day, so we time video releases in those 'golden hours' to get those shares.

To get the office excited about new content and secure those first 100 shares, we've done some crazy experiments at Ixigo. It's like a mini launch party whenever we release a video. We need 100 people to be as excited as we are about the content. That's another reason we stick to developing in-house talent for videos: everyone in the office becomes a

'Whenever it is most convenient for your immediate community to share your video, should determine the time to release the video.'

stakeholder in its success. At every video launch, a tiny celebration follows the release, and many times, this has got us the shares. In the early days of organic reach, the first 100 shares were enough for the video to get wings and hit millions. But today, organic reach is almost dead. Facebook, for example, gives almost zero organic reach to a video, unless you pay and boost your content (remember, platforms are in the business of reach). So now, the first 100 shares provide validation to spend money on content since it is attracting meaningful engagement.

Loyalty is earned

If you ask your friends or co-workers to share a video, they may share it once, maybe even twice. But, beyond that, your content needs to earn their loyalty. You need to ensure that they're waiting for the next video to release, and are excited about it. This is the first test your content faces, and if it can get through this it has the potential to grow bigger and bigger. To check if any video really did work, open any video on any platform and compare the views and engagement (comments, shares). The ones with high engagement beat the ones with merely high views.

BEHIND THE SCENES

'Ringing the Bells'

In our office, we had this big gong right in the middle of the floor that was used to make important announcements. For every video we released, we carefully planned the launch and, hitting the gong, we would celebrate the new video. I remember hitting publish and then running to the centre of the office to hit that gong and announce the new video, asking everyone to share it, and join us for chai and samosas in the cafeteria. We made sure the entire office was excited about the new videos coming out and always looked forward to the tiny parties that came with it.

When we released the 'Ixigo: How to speak Malayalam' video in 2017, we called a coconut-water seller to the office and announced that whoever shared the video would have chilled and fresh coconut water waiting for them. And boy, the video was hovering at a few hundred shares at five in the evening, and by 8 p.m. it had 4,000 shares! It spread like wildfire, and it was all organic reach. I remember the biggest video we did, after kick off and a period of 24 hours, was still growing at 11,000 views per minute! When we released 'Ixigo Glass' a video on a fake pair of smart glasses on April Fools'

Day, people were hooked to this new invention. We made a photo booth where anyone could get their pictures taken with these spectacularly fake glasses, knowing fully well that it was a prank. Everyone joined the fun, sharing it everywhere. We've printed badges, given out movie tickets, had chai–samosa, samosa–jalebi, chai–vada pao and ice-cream parties. We even got paper plates printed with the words 'Did you share the video?' We have sometimes even had after-parties – chai and samosa for the launch, and vodka shots if the video hits 1000 shares in an hour!

So the launch time of a video was decided upon by considering when most of our office folk were available to watch and share the content, and attend the tiny party. We learned it usually worked best after 5 p.m. on Thursdays and Fridays. And that became the best practice. So, if you're ready with your video or kick-ass, share-worthy content, see what time works best for your initial core group. Release it, and then you will know in the first 20 minutes if it has audience approval and engagement, and, based on that, you can strategize how to spend your money. Or better yet, it may surprise you with a giant organic curve.

When to spend the money

As a rule of thumb, you spend money only when you see engagement. If there are meaningful comments and shares on your content, then whatever money you spend to gain reach will multiply those numbers. If you just get views and no engagement, all the money will be burnt on merely hitting eyeballs, with no engagement, and will go down the drain. The first 100 shares will give you a clear idea about what direction you should take.

'As a rule of thumb, you spend money only when you see engagement.'

But this rule is not written in stone. If you believe the video is powerful and the initial traction wasn't great, then you can spend a tiny amount on boosting it, and test the video. I've done this sometimes when certain videos did not hit the first 100-shares mark quickly, but a paid experiment resulted in incremental shares. So, to spend money on any video for distribution, the best results come when you see shares or engagement incrementally increasing.

The most underrated strategy

Beyond the quality and share-worthiness of content, there's one more strategy, an action point, to drive more viewership. The only requirement is that you need to consistently work at it. And that one killer, yet underrated, strategy is *outreach*.

Make a list of all the communities, groups and pages online who would love your content. Make a list of journalists, bloggers

'Outreach is the most underrated strategy for content distribution.'

and popular 3 p.m. blogs (the ScoopWhoops and BuzzFeeds of the world – content we check right after lunch, hence the name '3 p.m. bloggers') to send your content to. It's not that every journalist or blogger you write to will pick up your content, but they are always looking for great stories for their community and users, and you may just land up somewhere at the right place and time. Draft a basic two-line message about the content; don't make it sound like a blatant ad or promotion. Frame it as if you're doing them a favour – say that they may like it for their community and that you thought you'd share this post with them. And then, meticulously send out the mails, messages and tweets. You'd be surprised with the results, all based on the power of your content. NDTV has picked up our videos many times for their homepage, just because a tweet was sent to the right person at the right time. Many of our videos have been picked up by Facebook pages, embedded in Quora articles, talked about on Reddit and shared by popular blogs, all because we did the exhaustive outreach.

'It's not that every journalist or blogger you write to will pick up your content, but they are always looking for great stories for their community and users, and you may just land up somewhere at the right place and time.'

This strategy can give you surprising results. For example, when we released a video titled 'How to Speak Hyderabadi', we reached out to all the groups and pages across Facebook which were about Hyderabadi culture – from NRI (Non-resident Indians) groups to local pages – and one such page shared our video and we got a million extra views and thousands of shares organically. Sometimes, page admins may ask for a small amount of money to share your content (everyone is trying to monetize); it's good to experiment and pay them to get those extra shares because it opens the door to a new set of viewers who would love your content.

Last, but not the least

From getting your video ready for every platform, and planning the initial kick off for those 100 organic shares, to spending money to gain more engagement, to doing exhaustive outreach, it's time to look at what's already your strength for distribution.

If you have a mailing list, great. If you have an app, send relevant user notifications. Share it on pages, groups and communities you are a part of. We've had crazy success with WhatsApp videos, for example, once we shared a video in our office WhatsApp group and asked everyone to share it in their family and friend groups if they liked the video. After a few weeks, we found the same videos coming back to us from other groups we were a part of.

One more thing

Always remember that all platforms you can upload videos to are in the business of giving you reach.

If you want them to give more visibility to your videos, you need to understand how different platforms work and how to make them love your content. YouTube, for example, is a destination video platform. You go to YouTube and search for what you want to see. YouTube is, in fact, the second most used search engine after Google. Facebook, Instagram, LinkedIn, Twitter and every other social media platform that play videos are destination hangout sites. You go there to hang out and videos play as a bonus. YouTube is like going to a cinema to watch a movie, while Facebook and other social media platforms are the cafes or bars you hang out at where videos are playing on screens everywhere. When making videos for YouTube it is super important to make them search friendly (search for 'YouTube SEO [search engine optimization] basics' and you will find tons of resources).

However, regardless of where you upload your videos, the platform will love your content if:

- You post regularly (the more content, the more value the platform can derive in terms of ad revenue)
- You post share-worthy content (the more engagement and time users spend, the better for their ad revenue)

DESTINATION VIDEO PLATFORM

YOUTUBE

(LIKE GOING TO A CINEMA)

DESTINATION HANGOUT PLATFORM

FACEBOOK, TWITTER, INSTAGRAM
LINKEDIN & OTHER SOCIAL PLATFORMS

(LIKE GOING TO A CAFE)

An up-and-coming stand-up comedian called me once to ask how he could reach a larger audience with his content. Now, regardless of the platform, posting regularly and uploading share-worthy content were the most important factors. Then, posting longer content on YouTube and making it search friendly and posting short bite-sized snackable videos on Facebook and Instagram became the strategy. At the core of organic success for your videos is the shareability of it, not deciding which platform to share it on. When we understand how different platforms work we can package our content accordingly.

With planned distribution, your video gets its best shot at survival. If it is shared by thousands, it gets its wings and flies, if not...well, it was an experiment. Document what you learnt and move on to the next video. I must mention though that the above distribution process is about blasting your content into the universe, and it better be share-worthy, authentic content and not a blatant ad. Let's dive into the next chapter about content versus ads, to see how to be clear on what not to do when it comes to producing share-worthy content.

Secret #8

Don't Make an Ad

Over the years, the one thing I've learnt is that content marketing is the exact opposite of advertising. When we're brainstorming ideas for a video, I'm always cautious not to make it seem like an ad. I've realized that the first idea that comes to my mind is usually the wrong idea. Wrong, because it comes from a place that has grown up watching movies and ads on TV. Only when I go beyond the first idea and dive deep, making exhaustive lists from constant brainstorming, that newer, more relevant designs emerge.

Content to me starts with an obsessive focus on the users. In my fights with brand managers across companies, I've come to realize that while brand managers are the

'Content marketing is the exact opposite of advertising.'

custodians of the brand and represent its interests, when it comes to content, we (the content creators) represent the audience, the users. The content must be in the interest of the users first, and the brand next. The user experience, right from the first second of the video till the end, will determine how they engage and interact with our content.

When we truly take the side of our audience and create for them, inspire them, solve their pain points, celebrate their life, help them express who they are or give them a vehicle to make the world a better place, that's when we see true engagement. They then make the video their own and take it forward by sharing the content with their peers. You know your video has truly gone viral when you see others uploading your video as their own on YouTube and Facebook. It's the content version of how pirated copies of bestselling books are sold at traffic lights in India.

They don't really care about us

Ads, by nature, have been put in the BS category in our minds. Whenever we see an ad, we switch channels; we ignore billboards and look away; we switch windows when we see an ad, and scroll past their posts. As an audience, we've become ad blind. Our brains have evolved to ignore them. Ad publishers get nightmares just thinking of how ad blockers are on the rise on phones and browsers. Every year the number goes up.

'As an audience, we've become ad blind. Our brains have evolved to ignore them.'

People in the business of making ads usually get unsettled when I go on the offensive like this. But the reality is that if you ask anyone about the videos they remember sharing with their friends in the last week, 9 out of 10 times, it would be a content video and not an ad. When we create content which attempts to make an impact on their lives and provide value, or help them express who they are, then we don't just get fans, we get brand ambassadors, evangelists, tiny influencers, who will gather around water coolers and talk about our content, and our brand becomes a conduit in making that happen. That's the game which we want to win at – rising above the BS and providing value first.

So, how do you integrate your brand in the content?

One thing I emphasized, right at the brainstorming stage of picking share-worthy topics, is that the brand DNA has to flow through the ideas. Not the brand, but its DNA. Figure out what's that one thing your brand stands for, celebrates or is aligned with. It's bigger than what you do; it's more about why you do it, what's the underlying purpose and brand identity. When all your ideas have the brand DNA in them and you've created the content, the next step is the subtle art of brand integration. My rule of thumb is that the brand must be part of the video, not as an interruption or plug, but as part of the narrative. It is to be included in such a way that it is required for the story and the video to move forward.

Sure, you can have it as a watermark logo on top of the video, show it in the beginning with the title, and end with it in the conclusion, but when we integrate the brand as part of the narrative itself, it works better. Also, in the end, be sure to add your brand with its CTA (call to action: 'download now', 'sign-up', 'buy now', 'join us', etc.) For example, when we created the travel hacks videos, it contained the brand

'The brand must be part of the video, not as an interruption or plug, but as part of the narrative.'

DNA of travel and was initially only about how to pack your bags, etc. But after a few hacks, Ixigo's features were shown as a travel hack itself. Or when we created the language video series ('How to Speak Bengali', etc.), one of the phrases was about travelling and Ixigo was shown as the solution. Or when we created a rap song, the brand name was used as the rapper's signature in the song. In all the cases, the presence of the brand was subtle and took the narrative forward. It did not exist as a blatant plug.

Ads need to evolve

I'm not saying that ads are bad. I'm saying that when you think content, don't think ads. Ads are more important today for driving conversions rather than building a brand (conversions are specific actions that are recognized as being valuable for your business that users take when they interact with your ad – like signing up to a mailing list, downloading your app or buying your product). If you plan to build your brand by way of ads, then it's an expensive proposition; and if you don't have big budgets then content is the way to stay relevant in your users' lives. As per the traditional rule, wherever user attention is, your brand must be visible. But today, wherever user attention is, your brand must be relevant. For example, every IPL season, big brands spend millions on TV ads, because that's where everyone's attention is. Now, if you still want to compete with big brands, you'd know that user attention may spike during a match, but user activity on Twitter or Facebook starts before the matches and all social media platforms see massive spike in traffic. If you create topical content, you can ride that wave without having to spend a bomb on TV ads.

If content videos are like marathons, building your brand and loyalty in the long term, then ads are like short sprints, and are driven by conversions. The more money you spend on ads, the more reach platforms will give you and the more conversions it will drive, if it's engaging enough.

But ads need to evolve fast because users have changed and you can't still be showing them the same old formula. Do you remember the early days of TV advertising when every ad used to have a jingle like '*Hamara* Bajaj' or 'Nirma, washing powder Nirma'? Ever wondered why? It was because before TV came into our houses, these ads were made for the radio, and jingles were the way to go. When TVs entered every household, brands replicated the radio jingles and added visuals to create a new format. The same thing is happening today. I hate it when big brands create TV ads and then start showing us the same thing on digital media. Also, see how ads of global brands are evolving today. Back in the day, just using a celebrity was enough, but today the conversation and the hash tag comes before the celebrity. Brands need to understand that ads need to evolve with the users.

'Content videos are like marathons, building your brand and loyalty in the long term. Ads are like short sprints.'

Two types of ads

There are ads which build a brand and there are ads which are purely driven by conversions. The industry phrase for the latter is 'performance marketing'. Any ad for which you pay only after you see measurable results are performance ads, as opposed to TV ads, where it's hard to see actual results right after your ad is broadcasted. So all the ads you see on digital platforms, which offer measurable results, like on Facebook, YouTube, Instagram, etc., are in the performance marketing category where the entire objective is to get that conversion. Experimenting with performance marketing ads can give you better bang for the buck if you're a start-up or are low on resources. Also, playing the ad game can be expensive if you have a limited budget. A TV ad, for example, costs at least ₹3–₹5 crore to experiment with. On the other hand, we've got videos which hit millions of views created with almost zero budget. Ads are also expensive to distribute, be it on Facebook, YouTube, Instagram or any social media platform. Ad rates are at an all-time high on these platforms.

How do we make ads then?

The way I see content versus ads play out, is that content drives engagement and ads drive conversions. Both must be made with the same share-worthy sensibility, but it's just that ads need to move faster and also talk about key USPs (unique selling point) of your product or service. Keep them to the point, BS free, authentic and think tiny mobile screens for production value and not TV. One ad, which I love, that defied all standards of time limits and format, and went viral, was the 'Dollar Shave Club' video. It was not your usual 30 seconder, but it was brutally authentic and on point.

'Content drives engagement and ads drive conversions.'

One strategy which makes content videos and performance ads work well is what I call 'engage and retarget'. If you keep releasing share-worthy content videos, which drive tons of engagement, you can then retarget your short 6–10 second ads to the same audience later. That ensures your brand stays relevant with its content and you get your return on investment (ROI) for conversions as well.

It's all about the CTA

When it comes to content videos, there's just one call to action (CTA) I care about: shares. The more people who take that action, the better the engagement and organic reach. But when it comes to performance ad videos, the challenge is bigger because, in my experience, there are two CTAs.

Every ad needs a call to action to drive conversions, that's your first CTA. But, if your ad has higher engagement from users (since the ads live on digital media), then your cost per conversion goes down, because the platform gives your ad a high quality score as people are engaging with it. Shares, then, become the second CTA. So the ads which drive people to take intended action and also drive them to engage with it are the Holy Grail, and that is worth experimenting with. One such experiment we did at Ixigo became a case study for Facebook, where an ad had 15,000 shares and the cost per install came down to $0.04. Also, when creating ad videos, be sure to have multiple versions to test which one is performing better and then divert your budgets to the best-performing one. The most important thing when it comes to ads, in my experience, is experiments. The more experiments you do with different formats and different features of the platform, with varied insights from data, the more chances you have of finding growth hacks. We need the DNA of rapid experimentation in our teams – another reason why in-house video and content teams make more sense as they allow for greater agility.

Secret #9

Experimenting and Return on Investments

While I was still new to the game, I realized quickly that experimenting with content was far more important than just pleasing one's boss or chasing targets. You can either match the expectations of your boss or join the rat race by attempting to match your peers, but real success comes only when you stop comparing yourself with others and start competing with yourself. To get better and better at what you do, experimenting must become a part

'Real success comes only when you stop comparing yourself with others and start competing with yourself.'

of your DNA; it must become the foundation from which you operate. The biggest successes in my career till date have been born out of experiments. I believe in this so much that in my annual review with my boss we have stopped measuring results and have started measuring the experiments we do. Of course, this doesn't apply to every line of work; but if you want to nurture creativity in your organization, the freedom to experiment gains utmost importance.

Experiment like a movie studio

As marketers, we're constantly shooting in the dark, trying to figure out user behaviour to predict emerging trends, seeing what could impact our customers or users. When an experiment works, we scale it up; aligning more resources for it and riding that breakthrough. My belief is that we must work like movie studios – make 10 movies in a year with the hope that at least two will click, and make the effort put in all the others worth it. Take a look at Yash Raj Films, India's biggest film production and distribution company. See how many movies it produced last year and then study how many of them were super hits. Every movie the company produces is an experiment to see what works. When a film clicks with the public, it allows the studio to get back all the money it invested, sometimes even a hundred times over. The key is not just being creative, but being consistent in being creative. If you're consistently producing, creating and experimenting with content, your chances of winning big increase. You never know which of your works has the potential to capture the attention of the entire world and break the Internet; but to get there we must approach our work like a scientist in a lab – by doing experiments. The more experiments we do, the better our chances of creating unimaginable benchmarks. Also, instead of chasing perfection in one experiment, how about we chase excellence while doing 10?

> **'Instead of chasing perfection in one experiment, how about we chase excellence while doing 10?'**

Get experimentation in your DNA

For a while now, the buzzword in marketing circles and LinkedIn has been 'growth hacking'. Growth hacking is nothing but aggressively experimenting across your company's verticals, connecting the dots, scaling them up and then chasing the next big experiment – thereby creating new opportunities. The people who are suited for such roles are the infamous 'jack of all trades', who were looked down on when I was growing up. Today, if someone has multi-disciplinary skills, knows a little bit about many things and can channel their focus to build what is required for an experiment, they are growth hackers. 'Jack of all trades' is now the new 'master of growth hacking'. A friend who heads marketing for a big MNC told me that they have an internal growth hacking programme, where they spot individuals with aptitude early on in their careers and then keep moving them from one department to another every six months, until they are skilled in connecting the dots and building solutions that span across verticals and teams. Sort of like how traditional Bollywood heroes were groomed – from acting to dancing to comedy, an all-in-one package!

The one thing I love about experiments is that they takes away needless pressure. When you're doing an experiment and toying with ideas, you find joy in discovery and creation. We live in a world where we're expected to hit sixes off every ball delivered, and that pressure is crazy. Every campaign will seem daunting when it feels like you have only one ball to play and only a six can save you. I say, forget this 'sixer off the last ball' mentality and enjoy the game instead. When you're enjoying what you do and focusing on how you can better yourself, you will be amazed to see how much you can accomplish. Shawn Achor in his book *The Happiness Advantage* points out that we chase success, hoping it will make us happy, not realizing that real success comes when you chase happiness.

> 'When you're enjoying what you do and focusing on how you can better yourself, you will be amazed to see how much you can accomplish.'

When you focus on increasing happiness, you end up increasing success. If you approach your work with a sense of joy and wonder, Mondays become the best days of the week, and you approach your work as a career and not just a job.

Experiments reaching millions

The biggest successes in my career in videos stemmed from tireless experimenting. We made a video experimenting with the square format and fast-moving content, which hit 40 million views in a week; we then scaled it to 120 million views spread over seven videos. We experimented with live videos, which resulted in thousands of comments on a single video. This gave us the confidence to create four more live videos, resulting in over 100K comments across four live videos. When we saw that regional-language content was fast emerging, an experiment we did resulted in seven videos with 3,25,000 shares and 24 million views. Our experiments with simple, image-based memes also paid off and reached 20 million users on Facebook. Once you see that a format works, ride that wave until others start copying you and the trend hits saturation. They can copy what you do, but they can't copy your enthusiasm in trying new things, and that, my friend, is the difference between someone successful and a wannabe.

Experiments in video formats

Here's a list of video formats worth experimenting with:

Live videos

I realized the popularity of live streaming when a video on Facebook went viral showing live action from the International Space Station in October 2016. It was something that caught people's fancy and was suddenly on everyone's screen. Later, it was revealed that the video was fake. Someone had taken hour-long footage from YouTube of the space station from a few years ago, and had played it on loop, streaming it on Facebook Live.

To create live videos, we need to understand the DNA of watching a live experience, the real-time nature of a live event. Unless you build that into the concept of the video, the number of people joining the live stream can be disappointing. Remember, you're not doing live videos for the sake of documenting something; you're experimenting with the format to learn what best works for you. As cool as a live video seems, for the user it shows up in the same newsfeed that is already cluttered and, therefore, competes with other videos for their attention. So live interviews or events don't reach millions unless there's a celebrity or a major brand involved, in which case there is an assured fan following that would be likely to tune in and watch.

For non-celebrity driven brands that want to capitalize on the live video format, the videos must have a real-time element to it. All videos must be entertaining, but for a live experience, it must truly capture the user's attention and keep them engaged till the end. For example, you could make a video showing the behind-the-scenes action of creating a live video, or, if you can, challenge your team to create a video while live, like a one-shot video, or you could do other fun experiments to engage with users.

An idea that we executed that got lots of engagement was a quiz that we conducted via Facebook Live. We asked questions, revealed the answers and, at the end of the live video, announced the winners. We called it the 'Great Ixigo Travel Quiz' and, as questions came one after the other, a countdown kept the users hooked about the next question, the next answer and the winners in the end. An experiment with live video must have, at its core, something people would love to watch or engage with in real time. A couple of ideas I want to try: Put a phone, with Live switched on, in a box tied to a helium balloon, with the phone facing the ground and release the balloon. As the balloon goes up in the air, so does everyone watching that live video. Or you could take all the reality TV game shows that have worked well on TV over the years and reimagine them for a live video format. We recreated a quiz show, which worked well for us. There are countless other interesting formats that can be done. The best part is that you don't necessarily need to work with tech teams to create such content. You can improvise and use your own phone to shoot live, and create some magic.

360-degree video

When the 360-degree video came out, it seemed like a game changer to us. We experimented with shooting a video of a car ride with a 360-degree camera tied to the top, to give the viewer the experience of driving through the city. (The 360-degree cameras have become cheaper can be rented easily too, for every big city has camera equipment rental companies now.) The result wasn't as exciting as we had hoped, however. Ninety per cent of the users who viewed that video saw it without experiencing it in 360 degree. They had just watched it like any other video, without tilting their phones.

In my evaluation of the video strategy, we tried to imagine people, busy in their offices or travelling in trains, watching this 360-degree video. To experience it, they would have had to move their phone and arms around, and would have been conscious of looking ridiculous around strangers. The bar for user engagement in a 360-degree video is a little higher. The content has to be spectacular enough to compel people to move their phones around, in order to experience the content, without being conscious of how they look in public. A little text in the video reminding them to move their phones would be helpful too. That's why the more spectacular the visuals are, the better the chance of users engaging with it.

Augmented Reality (AR) and Virtual Reality (VR)

Augmented reality and virtual reality have been marketing trends that hovered on the horizon for two years in a row without much progress being made in either. One reason could be that user behaviour hasn't caught on as fast as the new technology. Augmented reality (AR) is an interactive experience of a real-world environment where the objects in the real-world are 'augmented' using computer-generated information. All you need is your phone with an app that has AR built in, and when you point your phone at real-world objects it adds layers of information for your viewing experience. Pokémon GO, for example, took the world by storm; it is an augmented reality game that converted your environment into an interactive game. Virtual reality (VR), on the other hand, is an interactive experience within a simulated environment. It creates an immersive world when you wear VR gear attached to your computer or phone. For AR, you don't need additional attachments to your phone (unlike VR); so gradually, as user behaviour changes, AR has a higher chance of taking off as a marketing option.

Marketing experiments in AR may need some help from tech teams though. When Ikea launched in India, they did an AR experiment in Hyderabad, which was kind of cool. They launched an app that allowed users to experience how their products could transform a space – whether at home, school or an office.

Short-form content

Short-form content is exploding on millions of tiny screens across the country. If you analyse the most popular apps in India today, apps like TikTok are giving Facebook a run for its money. Short-form content (videos which are one–three minutes long) work well on social media mainly because they are snackable – that is, users need not commit a long period for it. It's a good time to experiment with short-form videos for Facebook, Instagram, Twitter, WhatsApp or LinkedIn, and with even shorter videos (15 seconds) on TikTok (which is hugely popular in Tier II cities in India). If you are just starting to experiment with videos, this is the format I would strongly suggest you begin with.

Long-form content

Long-form content, in my books, would be anything longer than five minutes. Anything which requires making a commitment to watch – videos we bookmark or watch at the end of the day, web series, interviews, TED Talks, stand-up comedy, all come under this vertical. The challenge here is to engage an audience that spends a lot of time snacking on short-form content and compel them into making a longer commitment. So perhaps, you can create short snippets for Facebook or Instagram, where viewers get an idea of the video, and you can keep the long-form video for YouTube. If you want to experiment with a web series spread over multiple episodes, you can put that on your YouTube channel or strike syndication deals with the huge number of OTT platforms (Over The Top, content providers that distribute streaming content on their own stand-alone apps) available today. Examples of OTT platforms you could partner with in India alone include Netflix, Amazon Prime, Hotstar, SonyLIV, Zee5 and ErosNow. With the popularity of such platforms soaring, thanks to cheaper Internet, there's a strong need for original content, and your branded web series could find a ready audience.

Regional language content

Content consumption in regional languages is becoming the biggest trend in marketing.

Move beyond the big cities in India, and you'll find smaller towns loom large on the Internet-consumption radar. Moreover, they are consuming most of content in their native languages. If you want to experiment with regional content videos, take a video that worked really well, find translators and copywriters in those cities to rework the script, and make the video in the regional language. One thing which worked really well in my experiments was to hire a local radio jockey, and get them to edit the script and do a voice-over in that language.

Songs and music videos

Music videos for songs are an exciting format to experiment with. Music videos have views in the millions on YouTube, perhaps because people play it on loop. You can experiment with creating a song (which is share-worthy) and a music video to go with it. In early 2019, hip-hop and rap songs were an emerging trend in India. Movies like *Gully Boy* brought the genre to the mainstream. So we experimented with producing a rap song in-house – from writing the lyrics to hiring an up-and-coming rapper for the vocals, to renting out a nearby studio for the recording and music arrangement. Once the song was ready, it was shot, edited and released in 10 days. It was enthusiasm and sheer talent that produced this video at such a pace, which in many organizations lies unexplored. It fills me with awe everytime I watch that video and recall how every team member came together to pull it off. Search for 'Ixigo Train *mein* Swag' to find the song.

Performance ads

One format that is definitely worthy of experimentation is the performance, or results-driven ad. Performance ads are the tiny video ads that run on Facebook, YouTube, Instagram and other social media platforms. They are usually limited by different time-limit formats and are priced differently based on how long or short the ad is. Performance ads work well to drive conversions (when compared to regular content videos, which are more about brand building), but ensuring audience engagement is the challenge. I plan my strategy to drive all actions in six to 15 seconds. Six seconders, or bumper ads, are the most challenging to crack and the most exciting space to experiment in. The 10 and 15 seconders come after this. My observation is that sometimes the simplest of executions can bring out amazing results. Many times, you don't really need to shoot anything for these ads. You can play with images, text animation and interesting, fast-moving visuals to make them work.

What About ROI?

Return on investment (ROI), the dreaded term all marketers' nightmares are made of. It's the one thing every boss around the world will seek only positive results on – how many products did we sell, how many apps got installed, how many leads did we generate? In my experience, the more experiments we do, the better our chances are of hitting the ROI jackpot. However, even for experiments, it all boils down to one thing for anyone who's spending money: what's the return on investment?

When I had first joined Ixigo in 2014, I was creating videos on my iPhone and had to really convince my boss about why we needed to buy a basic DSLR to make videos. After a couple of week of persistent follow-ups, I managed to get funds to buy the cheapest DSLR out there. And boy, after the next video hit millions of views and lakhs of shares, buying equipment was never questioned again! My point here is not that the DSLR got the video to hit a million views, but that the initial investment in basic equipment will even out in the end when compared with the massive branding opportunity that a video (which goes viral) can give you.

Here are three ways videos can impact your ROI:

Branding: If your video is worthy of sharing and attracts tons of engagement, you save money in distribution. Every share on the video, gets you newer audiences, increases the reach of your content and your brand goes further and further. Every person who shares also becomes your brand ambassador, taking your branded content forward, attracting his or her friends and family. You can spend money on distributing your content on YouTube, Facebook, Instagram or any other platform, but the best bang for the buck comes when it drives engagement. Also branding today is not just about recall and eyeballs, but about relevance and conversations. With every video you release, you can easily check how far it went in terms of reach, views and engagement. The more share-worthy your content, the easier it is for your brand to be relevant in consumers' lives.

Organic Conversions: One crazy effect of a video which is shared by thousands and starts reaching millions of people is how it impacts organic conversions. Organic conversion is simply someone taking the desired action you seek for your business without any ad spends. When your content starts spreading like wildfire, it results in conversions that start happening on your website, app-store or over calls.

Video Ads: Even though video ads are limited by time limit formats and may have different pricing based on how long or short an ad is, the best results come when they too start attracting engagement. When engagement on your ads (shares, comments, etc.) start skyrocketing, it also improves quality score of your ads and your cost per conversion starts to drop. We've seen that many times with ads which got thousands of shares – app-install rates dropped considerably. The more experiments we do in creating engaging ads, the better bang we get for our buck.

From experiments in video to ROI, the game of content is exciting. But there's one question I get asked a lot: this may be good for B2C, what do you have to say about B2B? Let's explore that in the next chapter.

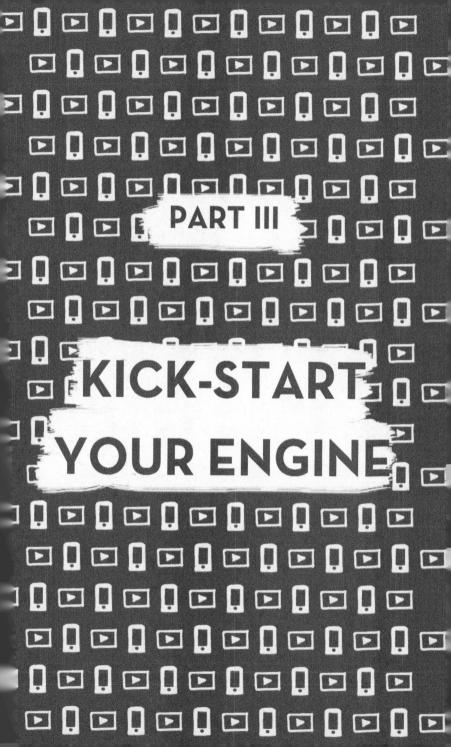

PART III

KICK-START
YOUR ENGINE

What about B2B?

One question I get asked a lot at events, masterclasses and the weekly mentoring sessions I hold is: what about content for B2Bs?

B2B and B2C are fancy-sounding acronyms to explain something very simple: who you are serving as a business. Is it end consumers (hence, Business to Consumer, or B2C) or is it another business (hence, Business to Business, or B2B). For example, SpiceJet selling you air tickets is a B2C business, but Boeing selling SpiceJet airplanes is B2B. For Zomato or Swiggy, the transaction of you ordering food is B2C business, but their transactions with restaurants is a B2B business. So, if any business is selling directly to the consumers it is a B2C business, but if it's selling to other businesses, it's B2B.

For any B2C business, the use of social media and content marketing have gained prominence, since user attention has moved away from traditional media to social networking apps. So it makes sense to engage your customers on Facebook, Instagram, WhatsApp or Twitter with share-worthy content, build your brand and drive more conversions along the way. But for B2B businesses, things haven't really moved on in the content marketing space. They are still looking at age-old case studies, white papers, infographics and blogs posts. Now, with video content taking centre stage on platforms like LinkedIn, the B2B world is waking up to this new reality.

'If B2C is about selling a plane ticket, B2B is about selling a plane.'

To hell with Bob

Remember the story of an American shoe company that sent a salesperson to India to see if anyone would buy shoes there? He returned with the insight that nobody wore footwear in India, and so there were no opportunities for growth. A second salesperson returned with the same insight, but with a twist – nobody wore footwear, and so the opportunity to sell shoes was massive!

Most video content made for B2B enterprises, in my experience, follow the same old formula: this is Bob, Bob has a problem, Bob used our product, Bob is happy again. I say f**k Bob! Nobody gives a sh*t about Bob any more. The audience has evolved, but many B2B companies are still stuck in Bob's world, peddling their product videos as content, wondering why their videos aren't getting any engagement.

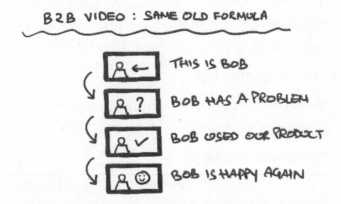

B2B VIDEO : SAME OLD FORMULA

THIS IS BOB

BOB HAS A PROBLEM

BOB USED OUR PRODUCT

BOB IS HAPPY AGAIN

Videos for B2Bs need to be reinvented and reimagined. It's not just about giving a product tour; it's about keeping your audience and your customer engaged. Speaking to several executives who work in the B2B space, one thing I've realized is that a typical sales cycle is about five months, and the value of deals in this space is also considerably bigger. It's not like selling a plane ticket; it's like selling a plane. Those five months for any B2B sale require regular follow-ups, phone calls and emails. But if your videos can keep your customer engaged, keep your brand relevant in their minds and conversations, then let the content do the engagement for you.

Never in history has there existed an opportunity where a social networking platform was built specifically for the business community. All the videos that brands made until now, either lived on its landing pages or were distributed as part of mailing lists. LinkedIn entered the picture and now it's almost like Facebook's business cousin, or as I say, Facebook in a suit. It's time to dominate on LinkedIn using video content. All the content you already have in white papers, case studies, best-performing blog posts, slide decks or as infographics... It's time to reimagine them in video format, tailored to suit tiny screens.

> **'Videos for B2Bs need to be reinvented and reimagined. It's not just about giving a product tour; it's about keeping your audience and your customer engaged.'**

How to create share-worthy content for B2Bs?

The myth about the B2B customer has always been that they are a very different animal to deal with, that it's all business and no fun. In reality, a person who uses LinkedIn may be active on Facebook or Instagram as well. We just need a business-to-business packaging for our content. The share-worthy IUCTC method can be applied here as well, because it is not about the platforms but human behaviour. If you truly care for your customer and understand their pain points when it comes to the orbit where your business operates, then you can brainstorm 200 ideas for content, all aligned with the Inspirational + Useful + Celebrate Their Life + Topical + Change the World method. As I shared earlier, your business may solve one pain point of the user, but it can solve or celebrate other pain points in the orbit too. Let's say you sell a CRM (Customer Relationship Management) software to other businesses. Your products help sales teams organize their leads and manage their process, but your brand is bigger than your product. If you deep dive into the pain points of users, you could create useful videos like 'How to Introduce Two People' or 'Five Ways to Close a Sale' or 'Things Every Salesperson Is Tired of Hearing' or 'Every Cold Call Ever' or 'Basics in

Body Language', and so on. The goal is to make B2B marketing fun; to make it entertaining again. And with LinkedIn your video content now finds a channel for distribution and engagement. When you keep your users engaged with relevant content, you're part of their lives.

If you scan every chapter in this book from a B2B lens, you'll find that the same fundamentals apply to B2B marketing too. From coming up with share-worthy ideas for content, to creating content for short attention spans, storytelling before production value, making content for tiny mobile screens, thinking of conversations first, figuring out your distribution strategy, to not making ads (when making content) and experimenting, all the rules apply here as well.

> **'If you scan every chapter in this book from a B2B lens, you'll find that the same fundamentals apply to B2B marketing too.'**

Invest in an in-house video team

There isn't a better time to invest in an in-house video team to power the video content strategy for your business than now. In-house teams are more agile, understand the core of your brand and business, and filmmakers often double up as designers, since they're usually skilled at both. Plan like you're running a marathon and not a sprint, and focus on creating as many videos and doing as many video experiments as you can.

Invest in your personal brand

When you invest in your personal brand and start creating content for LinkedIn, it helps in two ways. First, since LinkedIn is built around user profiles, it attracts the right audience, creates credibility among your peers and betters your prospects. Second, when you release new content from your business page, you can post it from your own profiles too, and that provides additional distribution, increasing the reach of your content. If even five people in your company have solid personal brands and a sizeable following on LinkedIn, it acts as a booster shot whenever you release new content.

What to measure and RoI

For starters, the only thing worth measuring with regard to content is engagement. The more comments and shares your content attracts, the wider its reach will be. And you can create short video ads, driven by clear CTA, which can then be retargeted to the same audience who engaged with your content earlier. When you create content which impacts and provides value to your target audience, you start to see people tagging their peers in the comments, and that's where opportunities lie.

Personal Branding: Kill Job Insecurity

If I could go back in time and give my younger self one piece of advice, it would be this: invest in personal branding! Having a personal brand frees you from the rat race, kills job insecurity and puts you on the path to purpose-driven success. If you're a student and have a strong personal brand, you stand out from the crowd at your first job. If you've got a job, having a personal brand ensures exciting career opportunities will chase you; and if you're an entrepreneur, it attracts the right partners, team members and investors. Personally, my greatest fear was always job insecurity, and I wanted to kill it by being known by the work I did and not the company I worked for. It's about creating an identity that is bigger than your current job or role; an attempt to be identified not by where you

'Having a personal brand frees you from the rat race, kills job insecurity and puts you on the path to purpose-driven success.'

work but by what you do best.

I meet so many senior folk at events who are incredible at what they do, yet don't share their experiences and build a personal brand. At the same time, there are those who do mediocre work but are great at PR and personal branding, and grab all the attention. When you're an influencer or a thought leader in your industry, opportunities open up, and give you the chance to build a career and not just work a job.

Oh, I can't brag about myself

All the people I've talked to about personal branding have one common problem to share: 'I can't talk about myself; I can't brag about what I do. I believe in working hard and not tooting my horn.' This is the biggest misconception about personal branding. In reality it's not about you. Personal branding is about helping the younger version of you – students, fresh entrants, young colleagues, individuals who are still struggling, figuring it out and climbing the ladder. These younger versions of you are in the millions across the country, and investing in personal branding is about creating content that helps them, using your learning, insights and experiences. Imagine if a younger sibling asked you a question about life or your career. You would naturally be inclined to respond to them with empathy and give them insights from your experiences and successes. Or look at it this way, if a newspaper asked you to write a column every week about anything under the sun, what would you write about? It would be about what you're most passionate about – things you know well, have experience in and so would be inclined to talk about. That's the content that will attract the millions who would benefit from your experience. A community, or a tribe, would arise from following your content and will help build your personal brand. Stop thinking of it as an exercise that focuses on how cool you

'Stop thinking of it as an exercise that focuses on how cool you are. Instead see it as a platform where you can help and serve others.'

are. Instead see it as a platform where you can help and serve others. When the spotlight moves away from you and moves towards the millions you can impact, that's when you gain a sense of purpose.

Thought leadership

Once you start creating content, become regular at producing it, and get active engagement and questions from your community, a point will come when you become an influencer (even if only in a small way, initially) in your industry and you can be categorized as a thought leader. An influencer is just someone who leads with original insights and thoughts, and builds a fan following by sharing content. As you embark on your journey of sharing, it will ignite self-

'Buy an expensive notebook and make notes of your learning from experiments, courses, insights from mentors, etc. An expensive notebook because when it costs more and the pages are limited, you're more likely to fill it with wisdom.'

discovery. You build a tendency to share whatever you learn. The more you learn, the more you will share; and slowly you start getting more clarity about your work and insights, and that regular exercise will make you a thought leader. Look at all the people you look up to in the industry – whose blogs you read or videos you watch for motivation. All of them are sharing what they learnt, their insights, and are truly helping others. Here's a hack I suggest to students who I meet for mentorship: go buy an expensive notebook and make notes of your learning from experiments, courses, insights from mentors, etc. Buy an expensive notebook because when it costs more and the pages are limited, you're more likely to fill it with wisdom and not random thoughts. And that notebook becomes a curated manual, filled with your authentic perspective. So if you want to become an influencer or thought leader, start investing in learning, start applying that learning, and share what works and what doesn't.

Speak more

One thing that really helps in building your brand is public speaking. When you speak regularly at industry events or places where your following is, your credibility as a thought leader grows. When you walk the talk, you're seen as someone with authority on the subject. Also the confidence with which you communicate to an audience often has a direct impact while creating video blogs. But public speaking brings with it a tremendous fear of failure for many. I heard Jerry Seinfeld once mention in his act that the number one fear people have around the world is public speaking; number two is death. But just like any other skill, once you start investing time in learning and preparing, you get better at it. When I was in Canada, my business partner suggested I join Toastmasters, a global volunteer-led organization, where you join and embark on your journey to get better at public speaking. Toastmasters meetups happen around the world, and if you check, chances are that you will find one in your city. Every week, the group meets and there's a clear agenda followed about practicing public speaking in a safe environment where everyone is learning. When you start gaining confidence,

'When you speak regularly at industry events or places where your following is, your credibility as a thought leader grows.'

you can start by approaching colleges and business schools to conduct talks for students. That's the best way, in my experience, to build your speaking ability. Then you can slowly graduate to industry events. Keep applying as a speaker for events, and, in time, you will start getting invites.

Hanuman effect

Of all the people I meet who are passionate about what they do, one thing I see a lot is a lack of self-belief about being in the public domain. I've met students who're afraid to speak up, entrepreneurs who are reluctant to write blogs and CEOs who are hesitant to appear in video blogs. But when I start asking them questions and get into a conversation, they are full of energy about what they love doing and they tell me they feel inspired to start creating content. They have it in them, and just need a nudge to start. I call this the Hanuman Effect. In the ancient Hindu epic Ramayana, Hanuman was a warrior who was reminded by Lord Rama that he has the power and ability to fly. And with that self-belief, he flew! I'm not saying you should also believe that you can fly and jump off a building, but you have your abilities and potential, which can help you fly, metaphorically, if only you believe in yourself. One thing which stopped me from taking action early on was a fear of failure and a lack of self-belief. Once someone reminds you of what you are capable of, it can do wonders for your confidence. That someone could be a close friend or even an experience you had, which encouraged you to share your talents more.

And finally, how to begin?

The first thing is to apply all the fundamentals I've shared in the previous chapters, all the secrets of content marketing that have resulted in millions of views and shares for me. You picked up this book perhaps to learn how to apply the insights to your job or business. Well, now it's time to focus all of that in creating content for your personal brand as well.

The first step would be to brainstorm with your close friends about what share-worthy insights you have. Start by listing the top 10 questions people ask you, because when you're answering questions you are your natural self. For example, I asked a friend who worked in sales to tell me three things he learnt from his first cold call. He began to talk passionately about it, and continued until I stopped him, informing him he had said enough to create a blog post! If you're good at writing, write; if you're good at talking, make videos. Head in the direction of whatever comes naturally to you. The rule of thumb is to create share-worthy content, which is fast moving, made for consumption on mobile phones and becomes a starting point for conversations. Your focus at this stage must be on content, rather than production value. Begin with something you can do on your own without anyone's help, and distribute it wherever you think your audience is (LinkedIn, Facebook, Instagram or any other platform where you think you can find your tribe). For example, take a look at the chapter about picking share-worthy topics and read it again with yourself as a brand in mind. As a brand, you have a certain DNA, something you stand for, and there should be clarity about who you can serve. Now if you apply the IUCTC method, you can create a list of ideas and start taking action.

For example, applying the same method myself, I posted a picture on LinkedIn, which in 5 days attracted 13,000 likes and 500 shares! It was a simple post in the Change the World category. It was a picture of a cobbler with text that read: 'Walking to work, I saw this cobbler sitting idle every day. "*Kaise ho?*" I asked; he replied in a dejected tone that nobody stops by any more. I wondered... Ain't that the challenge we face every day? People don't stop by, they don't convert, or engage.

Like an "aha!" moment, I ran to the office, fired up my laptop and printed a sheet of paper and stuck it to cardboard, with a little CTA. It read, "Remember to bring that broken shoe, chappal, sandal tomorrow!" I went back and installed it beside the cobbler. After a few days of travelling, I walked by the same guy on my way to work, and asked my usual, "*Kaise ho?*". His eyes lit up – his sales had doubled and now this little cardboard sign was part of his toolkit. So here's a challenge: in your daily routine, can you find that one person you can help, with the skills and knowledge you use every day at work? Post pictures in the comments. #BeTheChange'.

Become a self-reliant content machine

My goal in creating content for personal branding is to have zero dependence on anyone else. Whenever I have something to share, I should be able to produce the content and share it on my own terms. If you want to write, just start writing. Start by writing 10 posts, but don't share them with anyone. The eleventh piece you write will be in a form that is ready to be shared, with your authentic style. The game is to get better at writing, finding your voice and becoming consistent at producing content. When, for example, my dad wanted to create videos, I got him an iPhone and instructed him on how to use a simple app to make his own videos. My only condition was that he would review all of them with the same fundamentals I obsess over when creating videos. He duly created 10 videos, and finally shared only the eleventh with the world. Now,

'The game is to get better at creating content, finding your voice and becoming consistent at it.'

he's on his own – independently creating videos, sharing his insights and helping people who are still figuring it out.

For writing, I've learnt that we're better at editing than writing from scratch. I've applied this hack for my content. Take a topic and begin to speak about it, while recording yourself on your phone. Then give that audio to a friend or a college student looking for a short-term gig to transcribe it. Now, you have your article structure ready; all you have to do is edit, rewrite it in places, and you're done. If you want to make video blogs, one thing that has helped me is answering questions. Take a question, print it out, paste it on your wall and put the camera in front of it, facing you. You can look at the questions like you're looking at a person behind the camera and answer them. The trick is to not look at the camera, but *through* the camera. For someone who doesn't face the camera much, it can be quite intimidating to talk to the camera. But when you look through the camera, you're talking to that one person who's asking the questions.

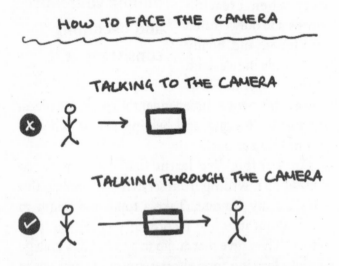

HOW TO FACE THE CAMERA

TALKING TO THE CAMERA

TALKING THROUGH THE CAMERA

When creating video blogs, you're not talking to an audience while on a stage. Rather, you're talking to one person who's watching you on their phone. Another way you could make creating video blogs easier is to use teleprompter apps. You know how newsreaders look straight at you and deliver the news – they haven't memorized the lines; they are just reading it off a screen in front of the camera. Let's say you write a blog post, you can next use a teleprompter app (search on the app store or Google Play store. I use Teleprompter on my iPhone and iPad) and read that text aloud. The text comes near the front camera of your device, and you just read it. This allows you to focus on how you say your lines, rather than what you say. When the text appears near the camera, it creates the illusion that you're looking straight into the camera, which allows the audience

'When creating video blogs, you're not talking to an audience while on a stage. You're talking to one person who's watching you on their phone. Don't look at the camera; look through the camera at that person and talk.'

the experience of you talking directly to them. Download some video editing apps on your phone and keep experimenting with them. Video editing isn't that big a deal, but it is an essential skill if you want to be a self-reliant content-creating machine.

How to make the platforms love you

There are two things I've learnt about increasing the reach of your content on any platform. You could start creating content for LinkedIn, Instagram, Facebook or YouTube. First, be regular in posting content. When a platform sees you posting regularly, the algorithms start liking you, because you're creating more value for them. And the more options an audience gets, the longer they stick to that platform, which helps their ad revenue. Second, create share-worthy content. When there is engagement on your content, more people spend more time on the platforms, which is what these platforms want. Also, experiment with making videos. Videos are exploding on every platform, and there couldn't be a better time to explore this. For example, I wrote an article on LinkedIn about content marketing trends for 2019. The article had 11 comments. But when I made a simple video about the same content (I read it off the teleprompter app), it got 38 comments and 15,000 views!

In the end, it's never about you

From the fundamentals of share-worthy content to building your own personal brand, in the end, it's never about you. It's about how many people you can serve, how many you can help. Can you be the reason, a conduit, through which help flows? A book I read once, *The Go-Giver: A Little Story about a Powerful Business Idea* by Bob Burg and John David Mann, was so great that I wanted to share it with everyone around me. I told my wife about it, my friends, and then I had a crazy idea. I posted on LinkedIn that I'd love to gift this book, which articulated values I loved, to anyone who wanted it. They just

'It's never about you. It's about how many people you can serve, how many you can help.'

had to fill their address in a sheet and I would courier it to them – plain and simple. Then I went to bed. In the morning, the sheet had 275 addresses! The joy of sharing and being a tiny positive impact in someone's life is beyond anything money can buy. I gave the bulk order to a local bookstore, instead of on Amazon and got help from my team to wrap and courier 275 books! And every rupee I spent on the whole thing, I got back in unexpected ways. One from a referral bonus at work, another when a paid speaking gig turned up. Sometimes when you truly want to do the right thing, the universe comes together to make it happen.

Last Words

In the end, it's never about the platform, production value or how cool your brand is. It's about how deeply you understand your user or customer. It's about how much you care about their life, and making a difference in it. It's about looking in the same direction as them, and not looking at them. Every successful brand, product or company is built on great customer love. That love comes from providing a great user experience, and when it comes to content, it's the experience of every second they spend with your work that matters.

Whenever I speak at events, I notice that the audience is always hungry for insights, tired of the craziness of fast-moving campaigns and of pleasing their bosses. I say, if you only takeaway one thing from this book, let it be this: go hug your end user (figuratively). If you genuinely care for them, they will come back, bringing millions with them to support your cause and brand and endorse your products. In the busyness of everything, we tend to forget who we are working for, and who's actually paying us – our users and customer. In my experience while working and consulting with many businesses, I've noticed that most people work to keep their boss happy. The boss works to keep the CEO happy, the CEO works to keep the investors happy. Investors say, keep your users happy. Why not focus on the user right at the beginning? If you prioritize user experience above everything else, they win, and you win.

The heart of this book is about the direction in which we need to focus, and not about the tools which will get us there. Once you're clear about what the right direction is, then you will find all the tools and help available in the world. From applying the IUCTC method of churning out share-worthy ideas, to tailoring your content for short attention spans and tiny screens; from prioritizing storytelling to starting conversations; from distribution checklists to continuous experimentation, my goal with this book was to dive deep and get to the core of outlining a proven process to simplify ideation and creation, and not just curate tips for different platforms.

Because, in the fast-changing world of business and consumer behaviour, having a process and continuously building on the method wins you results. It is a blueprint that I keep improving with experiments, and one I hope you can follow, to simplify the creative process – to kick ass with content that engages your audience, without peddling your brand or products through mere ads. The future is not in the hands of those who have ideas, but those who can execute them. Use this as a manual to catapult your brand – be it your business, start-up or your own personal brand – with the power of great content.

I'm with you on your journey of impacting a billion lives with share-worthy content. Whenever you get stuck, pick up the book and get to the chapter that can help, or send me a tweet or a message. I'll be sharing my ongoing experiments and adding learning resources on my blog www.aashishchopra.com. I'd be glad to help you on your path to success if you are committed to it yourself. Together we can make the world a better place, one video at a time. The best way to grow is to keep sharing what you learn with others who are also figuring things out. So share this book with someone who can also learn from it.

Together we rise.

Acknowledgements

You're never alone in your journey, there are people who believe in you, give you a hand and pull you out of ditches. Here are some rockstars who helped shape my journey and this book.

Maryann Taylor for always being my sounding board for ideas. You're the first fire test every thought I have goes through. And Fiona (our cat) for never giving me a dull moment and humbling me to treat you like royalty.

Mom and Dad for always being the rock solid support and giving me the freedom to pursue what I wanted – from the decision to drop out of college to religiously calling me after every million views.

Arjun, Sonal and family for cheering for every video release and sending me screenshots of videos being shared.

Johnny Ezekiel for teaching me the value of taking personal responsibility, taking action and always believing in me.

Rahul Dev for all the walks and daily conversations about all things marketing, always hustling to succeed, and for the many hours spent extensively reviewing this book.

Parivartan Kukreti for being my brother from another mother, the time we've spent having 10,000 cups of coffee in the last three years, validated many of my ideas.

Aloke Bajpai and Rajnish Kumar: You have built a rock solid company and culture at Ixigo. If you hadn't cultivated a freedom to pursue what we wanted, nothing would have happened. Thank you for making me love Monday mornings.

Anurag Dixit and Yashaswiraj Kamra for taking ownership, sharing the craziness of experiments and taking action. From the days I hired you as boys with filmmaking dreams, you have evolved into responsible and super sharp filmmakers, with a twist, of content marketing.

Team Ixigo for having helped in brainstorming sessions, acting, doing voice-overs, and helping in production and enthusiastically sharing the videos. The 100% in-house video swag comes from you guys.

Jayant Rastogi for transcribing text from countless masterclass videos, which became the basis of the book.

Sohini Pal and Prerna Vohra for igniting the writer in me, meeting with examples of books and writing styles I could pursue and feedback on how it would all pan out.

Ansila Thomas for being super patient with the writing process, her suggestions and for helping with the countless edits.

Poulomi Chatterjee for being the editor I always wanted, unforgiving with dedication to quality and always open to ideas.